7.14.23

EVIDENCE WEALTH

To Kyle,
Consider The Evidence!
Blessings,
Matt Gentry

EVIDENCE WEALTH

Investing Made Simple, Logical, and Worry-Free

JAMES N. WHIDDON AND MATTHEW L. GENTRY

BROWN BOOKS
PUBLISHING GROUP

© 2023 James N. Whiddon, Matthew L. Gentry

Cover design by Creative Joy Designs

All rights reserved. No part of this book may be used or reproduced in any manner without written permission except in the case of brief quotations embodied in critical articles or reviews.

Evidence Wealth
Investing Made Simple, Logical, and Worry-free

Brown Books Publishing Group
Dallas, TX / New York, NY
www.BrownBooks.com
(972) 381-0009

A New Era in Publishing®

Publisher's Cataloging-In-Publication Data

Names: Whiddon, James N., author. | Gentry, Matthew L., 1985- author.
Title: Evidence wealth : investing made simple, logical, and worry-free / Jim Whiddon and Matthew L. Gentry
Description: Dallas, TX ; New York, NY : Brown Books Publishing Group, [2023] | Includes bibliographical references.
Identifiers: ISBN: 978-1-61254-654-4 (hardcover) | 978-1-61254-655-1 (paperback) Subjects: LCSH: Investments. | Wealth. | Finance, Personal.
Classification: LCC: HG4521 .W45 2023 | DDC: 332.6--dc23

ISBN 978-1-61254-654-4 (hardcover); 978-1-61254-655-1 (paperback)
LCCN 2023933730

Printed in the United States
10 9 8 7 6 5 4 3 2 1

For more information or to contact the author, please go to www.EvidenceWealth.com.

*This book is dedicated to all investors who
seek to be wise stewards of true wealth.*

CONTENTS

Disclaimer ix

Introduction 1

PART I: The Market and Wall Street's Methods

CHAPTER 1: Understand How Markets Work 7

CHAPTER 2: Don't Try to Time the Market 25

CHAPTER 3: Don't Play the Market Lottery 43

CHAPTER 4: Don't Chase Performance 59

PART II: Evidence-Based Investing

CHAPTER 5: Own the Market 75

CHAPTER 6: Optimize Your Returns 93

CHAPTER 7: Manage Your Emotions 111

CHAPTER 8: Hire the Right Coach 127

CHAPTER 9: Focus on What Really Matters 141

Afterword	147
Postscript: Faith-Driven Investing	151
Acknowledgments	163
Glossary	165
Notes	171
Illustration Credits	179
About the Authors	183
Other Books by the Author	185

Disclaimer

While the publisher and authors have used their best efforts in preparing this book, they make no representations or warranties with respect to the accuracy or completeness of the contents of this book and specifically disclaim any implied warranties of merchantability or fitness for a particular purpose. Neither the publisher nor the author shall be liable for any loss of profit or any other commercial damages, including but not limited to special, incidental, consequential, or other damages. The contents of this book are for general information and are not intended as specific advice to any particular individual investor. See your professional financial advisor for actions that are appropriate for your situation. Always review a prospectus before making any investment in the securities markets and remember that past investment performance is no indicator of future results.

Introduction

"There seems to be an irrational human characteristic that likes to make easy things difficult."[1]
—Warren Buffett

In more than a half century of combined experience in the financial services industry, we have interviewed thousands of investors who've told us of their frustration with the constant barrage of confusing and conflicting investment information, hit-and-miss approaches, and exaggerated return claims. We must humbly admit that early in our careers, we, too, were caught up in the conventional-investing advice system with its "black box" secrets.

But our professional lives changed forever when we discovered Evidence-Based Investing (EBI)—an investing approach that analyzes factual and time-tested historical data and applies it in a systematic manner. That meant no more dependence on those who claim stock-picking clairvoyance and crystal ball market-timing prowess to try and outguess all other market participants. Now we spend our working hours providing the proofs that define the obvious objective choices for investors to make. Simply put, our mission is to rescue as many investors from the Wall Street minions and mainstream media as will listen. That's why we wrote this book.

When an investor walks into our conference room to ask us for a review of their current investment portfolio, we typically see at least one of these three common mistakes:

1. **They are taking unnecessary risks.** The most common example of this occurs when there is an *overconcentration* of certain investments in a portfolio—or a lack of proper diversification.
2. **They are missing out on the key optimizers of market return.** Many investors are simply unaware of where investment returns come from—or that they are basically there for the taking in the long run. Instead, they blindly follow the Wall Street "wizards."
3. **They are losing money to unforced errors.** This often shows up in easy-to-fix mistakes: paying higher-than-needed taxes or just having the wrong investment in the wrong type of account. Other mistakes are much worse: making The Big Blunder of panic selling out of the market. The refrain, "short-term thinking is the enemy of long-term success," is never more evident than in the investing realm.

Now, consider that if even one of these three areas in your portfolio is out of line, then your entire nest egg is exposed and vulnerable. Sadly, and most often, we see *all three* mistakes being committed.

What about you?

On a scale of 1 to 10, with 10 being the highest, how confident are you that you've avoided these mistakes?

If you gave yourself a perfect score, then you may be wasting your time. Then again, you may want to stay around and make sure there are no surprises. If you don't currently score yourself in the top tier, we fully expect your number to be higher after reading this book.

In light of this, we must warn you that some of the information presented in this book may be unsettling. You'll need to unlearn some concepts you likely thought were set in stone. We're going to take you "behind the curtain" to expose some of the tricks Wall Street uses—and you won't be pleased after you see them.

Beyond this bad news comes great news: investing in free markets means that everyone can be a winner. Yes, that means you and every investor can have a piece of an ever-expanding economy. The returns of the market are essentially there for the taking and, as Mr. Buffett implies, it's far less complicated than you might think.

Evidence Wealth is divided into nine chapters:

Chapter 1 is an important examination of how markets *really* work. Herein, you'll find several surprises to traditional thinking that you may have believed yourself over the years. We let the data speak for itself to instill great confidence in the free markets in which we are all blessed to be participants.

Chapters 2 and 3 critically examine Wall Street's popular methods of trying to outguess the market by timing the market ups and downs or picking stocks, which, as you will see, amounts to no more than buying lottery tickets. Chapter 4 builds on this evidence to show how these common short-term strategies lead to the insidious desire to chase performance, thereby causing investors to chase their own proverbial investment tails. This section of the book makes it abundantly clear how active portfolio management is a "loser's game."

In the second half of the book, we introduce the Evidence-Based Investing methodology in detail. Chapter 5 discusses the critical topic of superdiversification and the building blocks of EBI-portfolio construction. Chapter 6 shows how to capture the optimizers of market returns that nearly every investor misses.

In Chapter 7, we take a short journey inside our heads to be introspective concerning our attitudes about money and how to best handle the *emotions* that come with it. In Chapter 8, we then discuss the three disciplines needed to succeed in your investment plan over the long term. We also instruct you concerning the important task of choosing the right coach. Herein, we provide the "must haves" in any client and advisor relationship, plus the exact questions to ask when you interview advisor candidates.

Chapter 9 brings with it a discussion about *true wealth*, which involves much more than money. As advisors and authors, the content in this book concerns the most rewarding and important aspect of what we do.

Finally, we added a Postscript that deals with faith-driven investing for those who have an interest in aligning their faith with their finances. Devoted and enterprising financial professionals have done yeoman's work in this arena, and we look forward to sharing the topic with those who might be interested.

And now, without further delay, we are proud to present the *only* investment strategy you will ever need. We are confident it will lead you to a worry-free investing experience and enable you to focus on the things that really matter.

James N. Whiddon and Matthew L. Gentry

PART I

The Market and Wall Street's Methods

CHAPTER 1

Understand How Markets Work

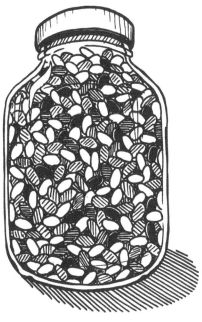

"Markets go up and markets go down."[1]
—Ronald Reagan, October 19, 1987 (Black Monday)

We believe that everyone can have a worry-free investing experience. That's because free markets are efficient, resilient, and prosperous for all.

When you fully understand these truths, it will transform the way you think about investing and eliminate needless concerns.

Let's start with our fortieth president's favorite snack.

FREE MARKETS ARE EFFICIENT: The Jellybean Experiment

At an event we hosted several years ago, a large jar was placed in the lobby, and guests were asked to estimate the number of jellybeans it held before they entered. The participants wrote down their estimates, and whoever came closest to the actual count received a prize.

There were thirty-five estimates put forth, and they had a wide variance—from 308 to 4,315 jellybeans. The average of all estimates was 1,759. The *actual* count was 1,776. Incredibly, the average had come within just under 1 percent of the exact number.

This experiment has been repeated many times with the average of all guesses usually falling within 5 percent of the actual count. How is this possible? Crowdsourcing. Simply defined, it's obtaining information or input from a sufficiently large number of people. And while only a few dozen people can have an impressive predictive record for President Reagan's favorite candy in a jar, what might the results be if we had millions of participants estimating the prices of public companies in the stock market? The answer is a highly efficient market.

Securities Are Efficiently Priced

The market is an efficient information-processing and pricing machine. Every day, millions of market participants all over the world come together and process nearly a trillion dollars in trades. Most of these trades are made by professional money managers, analysts, and traders who spend the bulk of their day doing one thing: consuming all the available information they can find on the stocks they're looking to buy or sell.

Each participant brings their interpretation of that information to the market, and a transaction takes place. The resulting price between a willing buyer and a willing seller can then be viewed as the most accurate estimate of current value based on real-time information. In other words, it reflects the collective knowledge of all investors in a particular stock. When new information becomes available, market participants are then forced to reevaluate their estimates and negotiate a new "fair" price.

As long as capital markets remain free to operate in this manner, it will continue to provide the most accurate price estimates through the most efficient means possible. Therefore, investors can generally accept the market price as the best estimate of actual value at any given time. Herein lies the cornerstone of worry-free investing. By embracing market efficiency, you put its vast shared knowledge to work for you in your portfolio.

Just as we saw with the jellybeans, we know more together than we do alone. You no longer need to worry about whether you're missing some critical piece of information because everything that is known about a stock is reflected in the current price. Investors who reject this premise are pitting themselves against the combined knowledge of all market participants and entering the realm of subjectivity (as shown in Figure 1.1). Good luck. They will need it!

Figure 1.1

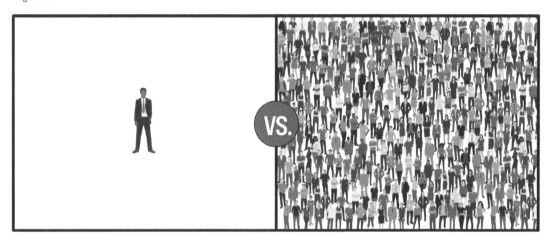

Markets Regress to the Mean

While counting jellybeans is a fun and tangible way of explaining why markets are so efficient, it also speaks to an important investing concept known as *regression to the mean*. In the context of the stock market, the idea of regression conveys that stock prices are affected by many factors over time. These market factors eventually work together to adjust extreme stock price valuations back to a mean—or average level.

In the jellybean exercise, the low "valuation" of 308 and the high "valuation" of 4,315 were obviously way off. As more estimates of "value" came in, the mean eventually prevailed at 1,759. The same is true of the market. As millions of pieces of information stream in, investors make decisions (buy, hold, or sell) that collectively combine to set market prices. This is why we will often say, "The market is always right—eventually." And with the scope of technology and rapid communication of the Information Age, prices adjust instantly.

Another characteristic that should bolster confidence in market efficiency comes with understanding how regression to the mean also buffers against extreme market events. Whether it be economic distress, political upheaval, war, or another pandemic, investor fear can be mitigated by understanding that large, sudden departures from the mean caused by such events are unrepresentative of how markets typically act. Therefore, a market drop is accompanied at some point later by a return to the mean. Isn't this exactly what we saw in 2020 after the COVID-19 onset? (Figure 1.2)[2]

Figure 1.2

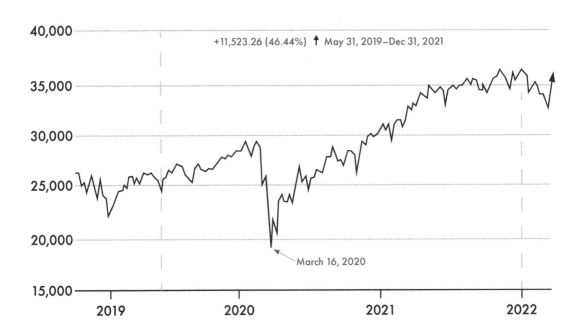

When President Trump went on national television on March 11 announcing a ban on all travel from Europe, it was a jaw-dropping moment. By March 16, the Dow Jones Industrial Average set another record, losing 2,997.10 points to close at 20,188.52.[3] That day's percentage plummet exceeded the infamous October 1929 Black Monday slide that started the Great Depression. Yet, just eight months later around Thanksgiving, the Dow was surging past 30,000 points. The Standard & Poor's 500 Index® (S&P 500) ended 2020 with an 18.4 percent gain. The Russell 3000 Index®, representing small US stocks, was up 20.9 percent. The market continued to climb and set records throughout 2021, with both the S&P 500 and the Dow reaching record highs on January 3 and January 4, 2022, respectively.

The sad part of it is that anyone who does not understand the regression to the mean concept will be tempted to make a move that seems right, but is instead the biggest mistake of all: selling out. Or what we call the Big Blunder.

The lesson: **get in and stay in.** Bad news and events will influence the markets, but their pricing efficiency allows them to eventually recover and regress to the mean, which trends long-term positive.

FREE MARKETS ARE RESILLIENT: They Win 3 to 1

Did you know that US stock markets tend to go up the vast majority of the time? In the last century or so, it's been up approximately 75 percent of the time. That's 3 to 1. In other words, for every one step backwards, the market eventually—on average—takes three steps forward. Figure 1.3 shows this relationship graphically over the last ninety-six years.[4]

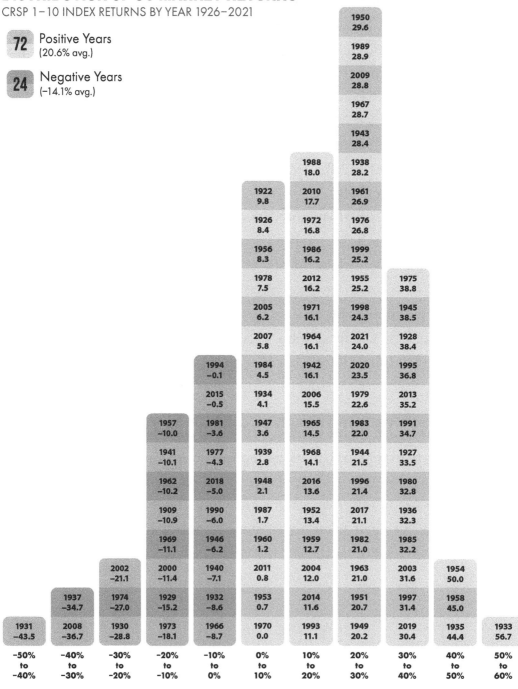

You will notice that in the years with negative returns (twenty-four), the average drop was −14.1 percent. For the seventy-two positive years, the average gain was 20.6 percent. So not only were there fewer down market years but also the highs were much higher than the lows were low.

> ### Happy Birthday!
> On December 31, 1984—ten days before Matthew was born—the Dow Jones Industrial Average closed at 1211. Thirty-seven years later, on December 31, 2021, it closed at 36,388. If the index grows at the same average annual rate for the next thirty-seven years of his life, Matt's grandkids can not only help him blow out the candles on his seventy-fourth birthday cake but they can also celebrate the Dow closing at an incredible 1,093,381.

Markets and Recessions

What about recessions? They seem to be in the news a lot. A recession is classically defined as "two consecutive quarters of negative GDP." What's the first thing you notice in Figure 1.4? There are more lines above than below. In fact, we count only eight recessions in these six decades. Only one of those lasted four quarters: the Global Financial Crisis of 2008–09. Notice also that only 31 quarters out of the last 250 "receded."[5]

Figure 1.4

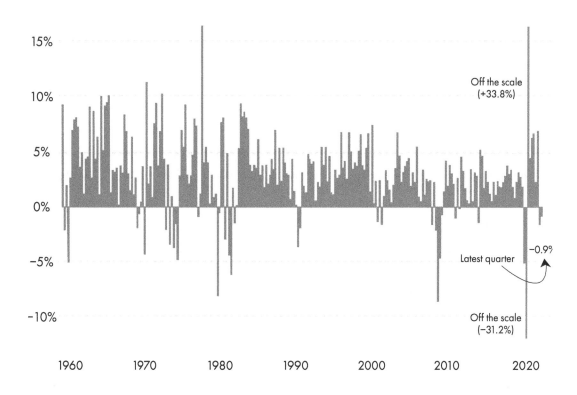

That means that since Jim was born in 1960, economic downturns resulting in recessions have occurred about 12 percent of his lifetime. That's not much when you consider the percentage of the time that the media spends talking about bad economic news. The fact that we are in a recession only about one out of seven or eight years is acceptable when you consider that the economy and markets naturally need this regrouping time of innovation to move ever higher in the future. So what about warnings we hear that, "It's not a good time to invest"?

Figure 1.5 shows that in the last two decades alone there have been plenty of reasons "*not* to invest."[6] But look closely . . .

Figure 1.5

SOME EXAMPLES OF REASONS NOT TO INVEST

Year	Event	Cumulative total return
1999	Y2K	467.1%
2000	Tech Wreck: bubble bursts	368.5%
2001	9/11	415.4%
2002	Dot-com bubble: market down −49%	484.9%
2003	War on Terror: US invades Iraq	650.9%
2004	Boxing Day Tsunami kills 225,000+ in Southeast Asia	483.5%
2005	Hurricane Katrina	426.2%
2006	Not a bad year, but Pluto demoted from planet status	401.6%
2007	Sub-prime blows up	333.2%
2008	Global Financial Crisis; bank failures	310.6%
2009	GFC: market down −56%; depths of despair	551.8%
2010	Flash crash; BP oil spill; QE1 ends	415.4%
2011	S&P downgrades US dept; 50% write-down of Greek debt	347.9%
2012	Second Greek bailout; existential threat to Euro	338.6%
2013	Taper Tantrum	278.1%
2014	Ebola epidemic; Russia annexes Crimea	185.6%
2015	Global deflation scare; China FX devaluation	151.2%
2016	Brexite Vote; US election	147.8%
2017	Fed rate hikes; North Korea tensions	121.3%
2018	Trade war; February inflation scare	81.7%
2019	Trade war, impeachment inquiry, global growth slowdown	90.0%
2020	COVID-19 pandemic, US Presidential Election	44.5%
2021	Omicron varient, China regulatory crackdown, what's next?	22.0%

Tomorrow is uncertain by definition. Unfortunately, as we've discussed, politicians and pundits use terrifying problems to stoke fear of the future to accrue to *their* benefit—whether for money, power, or both. Don't let this reality disturb you. If success and prosperity are never threatened, complacency sets in. Occasional adversity keeps companies innovating and looking for ways to improve their products and services. We like to say that "every challenge brings with it an equal or greater opportunity." This is true in individual companies, in the market, and in life.

The business cycle moves from peak through a recession, through the trough, and back to expansion as dependably as any other life cycle in nature. In fact, we like to say, "Gravity is the stock market's first cousin." Figure 1.6 shows the history of United States bull and bear markets based on the S&P 500 Index® with nearly a century of data.[7]

Figure 1.6

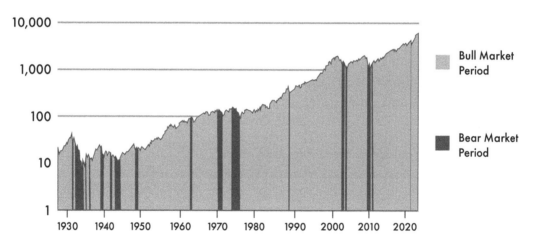

In the last ninety-six years, bull markets have dominated in the United States an astounding 87 percent of the time. As shown, the bull runs went up a combined 4,471 percent versus the market going down a total of 588 percent during the bear periods. Furthermore, the average gain for the 18 bull market time periods was 248.4 percent. This compares with an average loss of 34.6 percent for the 17 bear markets (defined as a fall of at least 20 percent from a previous peak). Furthermore, the 18 bull markets averaged fifty-five months in duration, with the 17 bear market retreats averaging only around ten months each.

There are two main reasons why occasional downturns in the economy are, on the whole, constructive:

1. A downturn tends to reduce and keep inflation under control.
2. A recession will not only discipline businesses, but investors as well. If people believe there will never be another downturn, you can count on them making bad investment decisions.

Of course, it's true that recessions have social costs—profits decline, unemployment goes up, and income goes down. And while we would never wish for them, they are inevitable short-term economic setbacks that have long-term benefits.

Sir John Templeton, the investment pioneer and philanthropist, once said, "The four most dangerous words in investing are 'This time is different.'"[8] We believe he was absolutely right. Yet investors who don't routinely study markets might ask, "Can we be confident that past market behavior will persist?" It's a legitimate question. That's why it's important to understand that the mechanism for changes in the market may not be the same as before.

Maybe it's subprime mortgages instead of war, or the failure of a major bank, or the health of the president; but economically, the ultimate results are the same. That's because free markets the world over must expand, and there is no stopping them. As we showed, the United States is 17–0 against bear markets in the last century. We don't expect that winning streak to end.

Market bubbles may blow up and then burst. But then the economy thrives again because of innovation born out of free market citizens striving for excellence. Simply put, the most important factor in getting out of a recession is always the regenerative capacity of capitalism.

Can you see why you should have confidence that long-term investing in the securities markets will be a positive experience? They are resilient. And the key to understanding this resiliency is to understand the effects that time has on money invested in free markets. For example, let's look at the results of the S&P 500 Index® (representing large United States companies) since the early years of the Great Stock Market Crash in late 1932. In the last eighty-nine years (Figure 1.7), a positive return in any single year has occurred the overwhelming majority of the time—again, about every three out of four years (76 percent).⁹

Figure 1.7

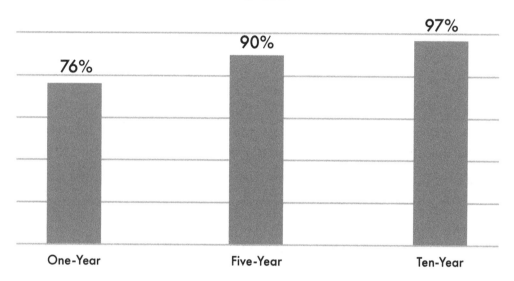

S&P 500
Rolling Time Periods
1932–2021

One-Year: 76% Five-Year: 90% Ten-Year: 97%

Next, we see how more time in the market mitigates negative years. When we look at five-year rolling time periods, positive returns occur 90 percent of the time. In ten-year rolling periods, positive returns occur 97 percent of the time. And when any rolling period of eleven years or more is observed, the returns have been positive **100 percent of the time.**

Furthermore, since the Great Depression (1929 to 1932), the S&P 500 Index® has never had another four-year period when it lost ground each year. The most recent three-year losing streak was more than two decades ago (2000–2002). However—just like clockwork—after this losing streak, 2003 came roaring back, growing a healthy 28.7 percent, which became the first year of a five-year winning streak. The worst year for the index over the last almost half century came during the Global Financial Crisis of 2008 when it dropped by 37.0

percent. That was followed by a nine-year winning streak and twelve out of thirteen positive years ending in 2021.

With this incredible track record in mind, consider all of the events that have occurred since the 1930s: World War II, the Korean War, Sputnik, the Cuban Missile Crisis, the assassination of President Kennedy, the Vietnam War, President Nixon's resignation, hyperinflation, Iran hostages, oil embargoes, Black Monday, the Persian Gulf War, 9/11, the Iraq War, COVID-19, and Russia's invasion of Ukraine.

Three of these events had a sudden and shocking impact on the psyche of the American people and on the securities markets. The surprise attack on Pearl Harbor was instigated by a rogue nation in search of global dominance. The Kennedy assassination was carried out by a supposed lone gunman of counter-political persuasion. The 9/11 attacks in New York and Washington were perpetrated by terrorist groups not affiliated with any single sovereign government.

While all these events were different, all threatened the very fabric of our society; and in the case of Pearl Harbor, even the existence of our society. These events had a negative impact on the stock markets. Figure 1.8 below shows the number of days it took the Dow Jones Industrial Average to recover to pretragedy levels.

Figure 1.8

Tragedy	Date	DJIA Closing	Days to Recover
Pearl Harbor	December 7, 1941	112.52	334
Kennedy Assassinated	November 22, 1963	711.49	4
9/11	September 11, 2001	8920.70	59

We can see that the recovery from these horrific events was relatively short as the billions of daily economic factors took control and overcame the negative effects. Capital markets are resilient even in the very worst of circumstances.

Correcting Market Corrections

When market volatility occurs, investors tend to naturally become anxious and ask, "When will this end?" The truth is, we don't need it to necessarily end quickly. That is, if we truly understand how markets work. Let's look at the evidence.

The following study of the last seventy years shows data on all the S&P 500 Index® market corrections. The peak-to-trough declines are documented to show how many calendar days it took for these declines to reach their end. Since the beginning of 1950, there have been thirty-nine official corrections (−10 percent or more) in the S&P 500 (Figure 1.9).[10]

Figure 1.9

DAYS IN DECLINE
S&P 500 Market Corrections
1950–2020

Date	% Decline	# of Days	Date	% Decline	# of Days
1950	−14%	35	1983–1984	−14%	288
1953	−15%	252	1987	−34%	101
1955	−11%	18	1990	−10%	28
1956–1957	−15%	194	1990	−20%	87
1957	−21%	99	1997	−11%	20
1959–1960	−14%	422	1998	−19%	45
1962	−26%	174	1999	−12%	91
1962	−11%	62	2000–2002	−49%	929
1966	−22%	240	2002–2003	−15%	104
1967–1968	−10%	162	2007–2009	−57%	517
1968–1970	−36%	543	2010	−16%	70
1971	−11%	103	2011	−19%	157
1971	−11%	76	2015	−12%	96
1973–1974	−48%	630	2015–2016	−13%	100
1974	−14%	29	2018	−10%	13
1975	−14%	63	2018	−20%	95
1976–1978	−19%	531	2020	−34%	33
1978	−14%	63	2022	?	?
1979	−10%	33	■ Corrections lasting longer than a year		
1980	−17%	43	▨ Corrections lasting between 157 and 288 days		
1980–1982	−27%	622	▢ Corrections lasting 104 or fewer days		

The average stock market correction takes about six months to reach the bottom. There's an average of one double-digit percentage decline in the S&P 500 every 1.85 years. This is a good reminder of just how common downward market moves are. Only seven of the previous thirty-eight corrections since the beginning of 1950 have taken more than a year to turn around. Comparatively, twenty-four of these thirty-eight double-digit declines lasted on average about three and a half months. From January 1, 1950, to December 31, 2021, the average correction was 188.6 days, or about six months.

Notably, since 1987, there have been only three corrections that took longer than 104 calendar days to resolve. Some experts believe this is due to the Information Age and the democratization of market access that tends to reduce uncertainty. This leads to a more rapid correction of corrections.

Modern-day corrections have resolved in an average of 155.4 calendar days (about five months). If you remove the dot-com bubble (early 2000s) and financial crisis (2008–09), the typical correction since 1987 has resolved in an average of just 74.3 calendar days (about two and a half months).

We know we're getting a little data-heavy here, but what we want to show here is that patience pays off in the market. Even if there is a longer correction, bull market rallies bring markets back relatively quickly. The free-market system is a wealth-building machine if you simply give markets a chance to correct themselves.

FREE MARKETS ARE PROSPEROUS: Everybody Can Win

How can we make this claim that everybody can win? Is that being overly optimistic? No. It's being *realistic*. And we're not alone in our beliefs. Great leaders such as Abraham Lincoln, Theodore Roosevelt, and Ronald Reagan all shared our faith in the people and ideals of capitalism and our great republic. They knew then just as we know now: free markets work.

To prove this, one would need only to examine one of the most profound economic experiments of the last sixty years: South Korea versus North Korea.

Figure 1.10

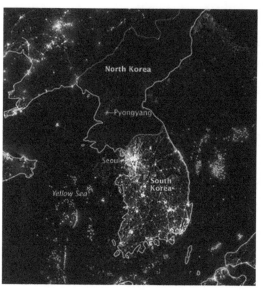

In this regard, a picture truly is worth a thousand words.[11] We call it the Glow of Freedom.

This satellite photograph (Figure 1.10) was taken at night over East Asia. The white outlines show the borders of North and South Korea. In the North, you can see the harsh reality of a society that has been devoid of the great economic opportunities that free markets offer. It's a society truly in the dark (literally). They are subdued by a regime of centralized economic planning via communism, and as a result, a severe shortage of electricity-producing capabilities. [12]

Figure 1.11

	North Korea	South Korea
Population	25,955,138	51,844,834
Infant mortality	22.21 deaths/1,000 live births	2.87 deaths/1,000 live births
GDP	$19 billion	$1.646 trillion
Electricity production	16.57 billion kWh	526 billion kWh
Exports	$1.85 billion	$606.71 billion
Telephones in use	7.2 million	94.4 million

By contrast, the vibrant free market economy in the South illuminates not only the thriving cities and towns but also is a shining example of what the spirit of free enterprise can accomplish in any culture that embraces it. It's truly a stark contrast between what government intervention in the form of regulation of prices can do (both for goods and markets) versus the system that allows the markets to find their own way. The lack of intervention (which ultimately drives economic growth) provides opportunities for individuals—and thus capital markets.

What more do we need to know before we have confidence to invest in the economic miracle we call capitalism? Will we still experience difficult markets periodically? Count on it. When? Who knows? And furthermore, who cares? As long as we have the system that allows prices to efficiently seek their own way, then economic growth will occur. With this in mind, shouldn't investors be most afraid of being *out* of the market when it goes to 100,000 rather than being *in* the market if it goes down to 10,000? In time, one is certain to happen; the other is not.

SUMMARY: What We Learned About Markets

Our goal in this opening chapter was to lay the groundwork so that you may have the confidence to fully embrace free markets to begin pursuing a worry-free investing experience.

Key Points

- **The free market is an *efficient* pricing machine.** The price of a stock at any given moment accurately reflects all the known information about it. In this regard, you might even say "the market is always right" in the setting of stock prices.
- **The free market is remarkably *resilient*.** Economic recessions and market corrections are short-lived and far less common than most investors perceive. Stock prices are affected by many factors, which can sometimes cause extreme and unusual stock price valuations. Yet, eventually, they regress to a mean—or average level.
- **The free market brings *prosperity to all*.** While we can't depend on every day, month, or year being positive, over the past century, the market has essentially taken three steps forward and one step back on average.

No other nation or economic system has ever existed like the one we are blessed to be a part of now. In light of the evidence, *optimism* is the only logical reality. You don't ever again have to mistake short-term market variability for loss because you now understand how you can have a positive investing experience through long-term positive market change.

Next, just because you now know more about how markets really work doesn't mean you won't be tempted to try and outguess it. The Wall Street minions and their media accomplices are all too eager to lead you in that direction. In Chapter 2, we'll take you behind the curtain of their "latest and greatest" methods to make sure you can ignore them and stay on the straight and narrow path to investment success.

CHAPTER 2

Don't Try to Time the Market

"October is one of the peculiarly dangerous months to speculate in stocks. The others are July, January, September, April, November, May, March, June, December, August, and February."[1]

—Mark Twain

When you visit our office, you will notice in the reception area a crystal ball sitting front and center on a small table between two guest chairs. Leaning conspicuously against its base is a sign which reads, "Out of Order." The message conveyed is unmistakable because . . .

Humans can't predict the future.

We all know this on an intellectual level, yet so many seem to believe it's different in the realm of investing. They yearn for the guru with unique insights that will enable them to analyze the billions of daily factors and predict accurately the direction of the market at just the right moment. Wall Street accommodates this approach—irrational and short-term though it may be. The simple truth is that no one can know where the markets are going.

We learn at an early age that "hindsight is 20/20." There's a behavioral economics term related to this known as *hindsight bias*: the concept that we can predict future events based on the information we have concerning past events. Yet a disclaimer, such as "past performance is no guarantee of future results," is required by law on investment literature and prospectuses. This is because, absent dumb luck, there's no way to accurately call races that have yet to be run.

Remember watching *The Wizard of Oz* as a child? Perhaps you recall that moment when Dorothy and her ragtag group of traveling companions finally reach the Emerald City and stand trembling in the presence of the Wizard—that seemingly omnipotent power they've never seen nor heard who holds their fate in his hands. Then Toto gets curious.

"Pay no attention to that man behind the curtain!" came the booming voice.[2]

It was a mixture of relief and a strange disappointment when the Wizard turns out to be nothing more than a nervous little man hiding behind a curtain. Likewise, Wall Street often tries to wow unassuming investors with the "wizardry" of their methodologies kept tucked away where only they have access.

TIMING THE MARKETS: Why Do Investors Try?

Market timing is the unstable foundation of an ineffective investment philosophy known as *active portfolio management*. The word *active* is often misconstrued as having a positive connotation. After all, investors expect their investment managers to *do something*. They certainly don't want them to sit around and do nothing. However, data shows that the more active a broker is with an account, the less likely positive things will occur.

The idea that markets can be timed successfully to benefit the long-term goals of the average investor is perhaps the easiest investing untruth to lay bare. Yet many investors believe timing the market is possible. Why is this?

REASON #1: Asymmetric Aversion to Loss

Fear is perhaps the greatest motivator in life. For investors, the desire to find some way to avoid a perceived great danger that besets the market is natural. Technically, this is called eliminating *market risk*. The trouble is, market risk cannot be avoided. That's the bad news. The good news is that it doesn't have to be. Unfortunately, market risk is just the kind of fear Wall Street loves to play on. (Perhaps you've heard the phrase, "Never let a crisis go to waste.")

The fear of losing money is exacerbated by a concept known as *asymmetrical aversion to loss*. It's a fear we all must deal with. Simply put, when directly compared or weighted against each other, losses loom larger than gains. Some research has put that "looming" at two to three times larger. For example, if the Dow Jones Industrial Average is up 500 points, you might feel good about the market that day. But if you see a *red* 500 on your stock-market phone app, you feel much worse about that down day comparatively speaking. This asymmetry between the reaction to the ups and downs as markets move through natural—and necessary—cycles often results in an unfounded range of emotions from elation to panic (Figure 2.1).

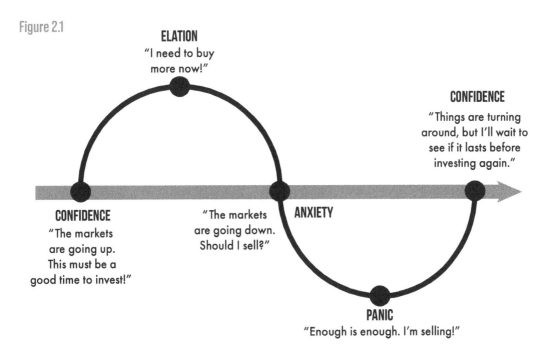

Investors who struggle to separate their emotions from their investment decisions most often buy high and sell low. A prime example of this in modern market history was during the Global Financial Crisis of 2008 as many investors fled to cash in early 2009. They locked in their losses just before the market rebound and had to experience the regret of watching markets climb to new record highs. Earlier, we showed a similar, but shorter, example in 2020 with the precipitous drop during the early days of the COVID-19 pandemic in February/March of 2020, followed by a record run-up in equity markets (Figure 1.2). Maintaining discipline through rising and falling markets is not easy from an emotional standpoint, but we'll show you how it greatly enhances your opportunity for investment success.

Here is the immutable reality in securities markets: extremely good and extremely bad circumstances rarely stay that way for long because supply and demand continuously adapt in free markets. While markets sometimes fall and rise rapidly, long-term growth is about patience.

REASON #2: "Beating the Market"

The "bandwagon" was born in 1848. During the campaign of presidential candidate Zachary Taylor, a circus clown invited him to board a wagon that actually had a band ensemble performing on it. Taylor gained momentum as a candidate, and thus "getting on the bandwagon" was coined. Taylor's electoral victory spurred others to try it in the future, and it became standard campaign fare.

Many investors are not so concerned about a market decline as they are taking advantage of perceived opportunities to capitalize on moments of profitable timing, or "jumping on the bandwagon." In our modern vernacular, we might also call it Fear of Missing Out (FOMO). The bandwagon effect might go a long way in explaining why short-term market fluctuations occur as the tribal instinct of investors kicks in. But both terms describe another universal human characteristic that Wall Street plays upon. If they can't get you by scaring you with the catastrophe du jour, they will try to appeal to your intense desire for wealth, or the hope of "beating the market."

Yet investors who obsess about maximizing their portfolio returns ignore the idea that there is a direct relationship between the frequency of trading an account versus account performance. Nobel Prize-winning Evidence-Based Investing pioneer Eugene Fama says it like this, "Your money is like a bar of soap—the more you handle it, the less you'll have."[3]

Regardless of the reason for seeking an investment strategy that outwits the invisible crowds of the free capital market, we will show that the evidence is clear. It can't be done consistently in the long run. Unfortunately, it's not just Wall Street minions that are trying to move your emotions.

REASON #3: The Media's Role

Market timing is a media darling. Nearly every major financial publication and broadcast in the country is based, at least in part, upon the premise that successfully timing the market is not only possible, but expected. "Why You Should Own Technology Stocks Now" and "The Coming Market Boom (or Bust)" are examples of common headlines that attract investors like moths to a porch light on a warm summer evening.

And why not? The media's business model is straightforward. Whether mainstream or social media, their job is to get eyeballs and followers, which translate into advertising dollars. That's it. Reporting the news or opinions of the day in a way that attracts the most attention clearly benefits a network or publication's bottom line. What better way to garner attention concerning viewers' nest eggs than to maintain either a "Get out while you can!" or "Don't miss out!" posture? Remember, the Weather Channel doesn't send a reporter out to chase rainbows. The path of the storms draws viewership. It's the same with financial markets. The uncertain direction of the market gets the attention.

One of the other main factors that aids the media's effectiveness is through a persuasive technique known simply as *repetition*. Repeating simple phrases or concepts can convince an audience they are true. People naturally take repetition as a social cue—especially in large group settings like in television advertisements or programs or in social media—because we believe the rest of the listeners might believe it. This makes investors vulnerable to making decisions based on information that may lack credibility, most often due to its incomplete or general nature. But whether information is right or wrong, the more we hear it, the more likely we are to believe it.

This also helps explain why the largest corporate voices in the financial services industry are the most influential. They understand the impact they can have with their well-funded megaphone that forms the beliefs and behaviors of the vast majority of investors through advertising blitzes with their compliant media partners.

Compounding the issue of financial advice via mass communication is that it is almost always far too general in nature to be valuable. Every serious investor needs *personalized* financial advice based on their goals and their unique situation. It's not hard to understand why investors make poor decisions when they rely on the daily newscasts, blogs, or TV programs for their investment advice.

When investors are reminded of what the media's role really is—to maximize viewers that translate into ratings—then avoiding the trap of accepting their reports as advice can be achieved. Thus, when investors scrub their media feeds of financial talking heads, they take a major step to being freed from the market-timing temptation.

TIMING METHODS: Technical Analysis (Charting)

There are a multitude of methods Wall Street vendors will use to try and impress the idea upon unsuspecting investors that they have secrets in their black box that either (a) no one else can offer, or (b) no one does it better than they.

One common tool used to time market sectors and individual securities is known as *technical analysis*, which involves making and interpreting stock charts. (Those who engage in this activity are sometimes called *chartists*.) Technical analysis is something we see quite often in newsletters and blogs dedicated to timing. These publications claim that charting offers a scientific way to make logical market decisions.

In a discussion of technical analysis, they might talk about a "bullish trend" or an "upward movement" in a stock price or sector, as seen in Figure 2.2. A "bearish trend" heads in the opposite direction.

Figure 2.2

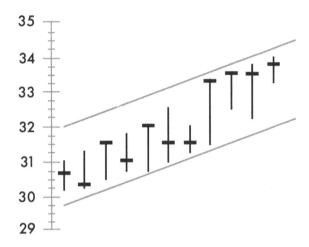

Or perhaps we would hear about the "shoulders" formed from the market's up-and-down movements that eventually form a "neckline." Breaking the neckline is said to be a bearish signal (see Figure 2.3).

Figure 2.3

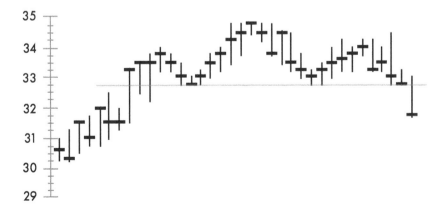

Technical analysis and the charts that go with it is supposedly just a matter of connecting the dots to find distinguishable patterns of prices on which to make predictions. All of this is designed to bring about a feeling that some detailed work and analysis has taken place. But the bottom line does not change: no one can predict the future.

Furthermore, these tracking techniques are designed to appeal to investors who are more interested in profits from daily trading versus long-term investing. But either way, this is a failed strategy for two primary reasons:

1. **No secrets.** There is a concept known as the *efficient analyst paradox*. Its logical conclusion is that the work of many highly skilled securities analysts will ensure efficient market prices, thus making those same skilled analysts unable to consistently find undervalued stocks. That is, a buy or sell indicator is of little value when everyone is acting on the same information.
2. **Randomness.** The chartist relies on their ability to read changes in direction or status of a stock price or market sector. But the fact is, the price of a stock is dependent on many random factors that occur somewhat rapidly—usually *very* rapidly.

Even if charts are coded and analyzed rigorously, they produce little or no statistical basis for consistently outperforming the market. They are simply a tangible illustration of wishful thinking.

Chartists' reliance on the momentum to change before making a trading decision creates the equivalent of calling heads or tails correctly twice in a row on a regular basis. They must know when to get in the market and when to get out. Or, when to get out, and then when to get back in. If they miss in either direction, the strategy fails.

Data Mining

Data mining—or back testing—is another common technique among market timers. Sometimes called *data snooping*, it's a methodology that can look very much like a credible way of arriving at investment decisions. For example, data miners might consider factors such as prevailing interest rates or industrial production in relation to stock market performance over an extended period.

If you're a pro-football fan, you may recall an instance of data mining that was well publicized years ago when it was discovered that each time the NFC team defeated the AFC team in the Super Bowl, we could expect an up year in the stock market. If the AFC team was the winner, the stock market would be a loser. Where did this crazy notion come from? Well, for several years the pattern held true, and thus someone noted it.

When it comes to data mining, almost anything can be used to prove a point. Others have referenced hemlines, sunspots, butter production in Bangladesh, and even factory emission clouds over China as possible indicators of market direction.

With many charts and graphs at their side, data miners will try to make a compelling case for an important investment move or strategy. However, at their core, data miners still are involved with the dubious notion of market timing and have little or no consistent evidence to support a claim that their methods work reliably over the long term.

Fibonacci—The Wizard Behind the Curtain

The Fibonacci retracement is an example of a tool used by technical traders and is based on the numbers identified by the thirteenth-century Italian mathematician. (You may recall the name from the 2006 movie *The DaVinci Code*.) He was also known as Leonardo of Pisa. The tool utilizes the mathematical relationships between the numbers in Fibonacci sequences.

Here is a brief sampling: it takes the extreme points on a stock chart, such as the low and high price levels of a long-term trend, and divides the vertical distance between them by the Fibonacci ratios of 23.6%, 38.2%, 50%, 61.8%, and 100%. Once the ratio levels are identified, horizontal lines representing the ratio levels are drawn on a chart, indicating possible support (price stops going lower) and resistance (price stops going higher) levels. In the Fibonacci sequence of numbers, each number is approximately 1.618 times greater than the preceding number. For example, 21/13 = 1.615 while 55/34 = 1.618 . . . and so on and so forth.

Get it? We don't either. That's the point.

We are guessing you've never heard of Signor Fibonacci. But this is the type of absurdity cloaked in big technical terms that is replete in the market-timing world.

Perhaps you've been to Fibonacci's hometown of Pisa, Italy. It's about as quaint and historic of a place as you would want in any European vacation destination. But if this method really worked, wouldn't you wonder why investment gurus wouldn't just use it for themselves and buy their own Italian villa?

THE REAL COST OF TIMING: Missing Out

When markets get choppy, it's common for jittery investors to ask, "Should I get out?"

Let's look at the evidence to understand how to answer that question.

First things first: we must always remind ourselves that short-term thinking is the enemy of long-term success. Therefore, anytime an anxious feeling about the market rears its head, we return to the data to reinforce why we should avoid the Big Blunder (i.e., getting out of the market) at all costs.

Figure 2.4 shows the results of missing just a few days of the best returns in the market as represented by the S&P 500 Index® over a recent thirty-year period.⁴ Keep in mind that these three decades include crises such as 9/11, the Global Financial Crisis, and the COVID-19 pandemic lockdown of the economy.

Figure 2.4

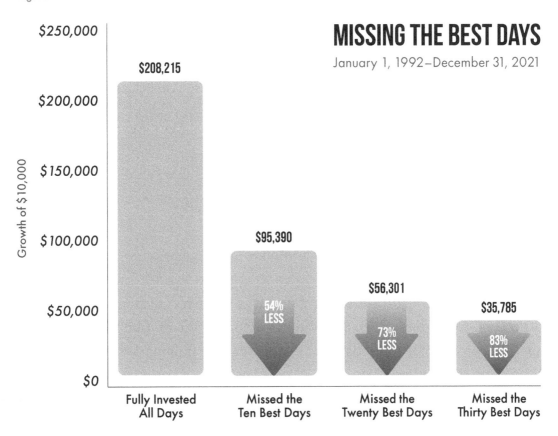

If you had started with $10,000 (nontaxable) and stayed invested all 7,556 market trading days, you would have seen more than a twenty-fold increase in your money. However, if you had missed only the best *ten* trading days over this thirty-year period, you would have forfeited *more than half*—54 percent—of your account. When we further consider the losses for missing the best twenty or thirty days . . . well, it gets even uglier as up to 83 percent of the return vanishes.

For most investors, the "Missing the Best Days" is shocking enough. Yet the data is even more compelling when we look at *when* the fifty best days occurred within the 1992–2021 period (Figure 2.5).[5]

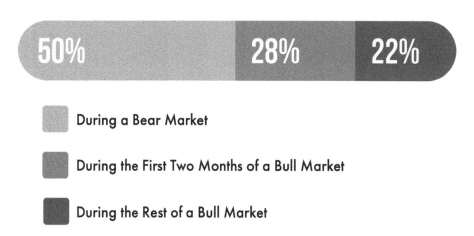

Figure 2.5

Notice that *half* of the best return days occurred during bear markets. Another 28 percent occurred in the first two months of a bull market—with only 22 percent of the best days occurring during a bull market run.

What's the implication?

That, ironically, market timers who intentionally sought to avoid bear markets—if they were successful—*missed out* on 50 percent of the best days. Additionally, mistiming their reentry into the market even by just sixty days would have cost them another 28 percent of the best fifty days. Contrast this with simply staying invested to get the full market return and *100 percent* of the best days.

Understanding this concept explains why market timers are so unsuccessful even when they "get it right." It's no wonder so many investors get frustrated when their portfolios lag behind the market when they supposedly have a market "expert" watching it for them.

Thus we believe the answer to the "Should I get out?" question is always "Never." The risk of being out of the market is far greater than being in it. Because of inflation, cash always becomes worth less over time. Good companies (stocks) typically become worth more over time. So as difficult as it may be psychologically to remain fully invested during difficult world, political, and economic events, that's what prudent investors do.

They get in and stay in; they *don't miss out*.

Right Time to Invest

So far, we've offered a good amount of evidence for why you should remain invested to ensure you won't miss the best days of the market. But what if you're not currently fully invested in the market?

When is the best time to get *in* the market?

Let's try to explain by remembering a tragic moment from over two decades ago.

The plane crash that took the life of John F. Kennedy Jr., his wife, and her sister occurred on July 16, 1999. Because Kennedy was not instrument rated as a pilot, vision was the dominant sense he relied on for orientation. Just before the accident, his plane was descending over water, nearing darkness, with otherwise poor visibility. The official investigation concluded that he fell victim to a condition known as *spatial disorientation*, which greatly limited his ability to determine the attitude, altitude, or speed of the aircraft. While he had instruments that could have saved him, his lack of training likely confused what he saw on his dashboard as the plane was lost to the sea.[6] It was another sad chapter for a family that has had more than their share of heartbreak over the decades.

As investors, we, too, can have a sort of market disorientation where things look to be certain in one way, but the "instrument data" is telling us something we can't quite understand. For example, intuitively, we tend to think that the best time to invest is always after a sharp decline in the market. Contrasting this, most investors are reticent to put money into the market after a big run-up. These common notions are the essence of "timing the market."

Figure 2.6 shows the performance of markets after monthly declines of at least 10 percent from the previous month as represented by the S&P 500 Index® since 1926.[7] Results are shown for one-, three-, and five-year annualized periods. As we might expect, the returns are very strong.

Figure 2.6

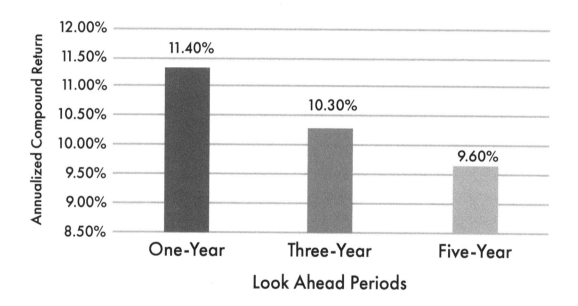

Presumably, if we could time it such that we could identify all the 10 percent declines in the market and invest then, we would we be in great shape. So this must be the answer to the question, right? Not so fast.

The next chart (Figure 2.7) uses the same methodology to show the performance after new market *highs*.[8] We must admit—even as professionals, we become a bit disoriented each time we study this phenomenon—that even *higher* performance occurred after record highs.

Figure 2.7

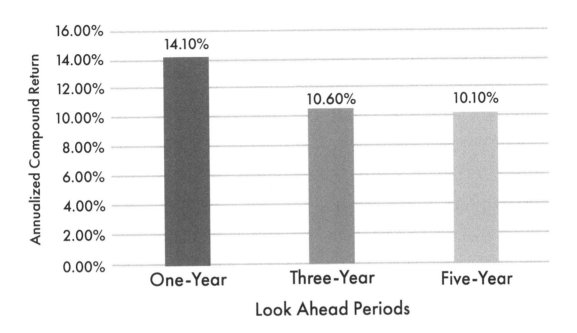

On the other hand, when we consider that there is approximately a 75 percent chance that the market goes up versus down, this makes perfect sense. With a 3 to 1 relationship, any time you get into the market, chances are it is going up versus down. Again, it's like taking the proverbial three steps forward and one step back. Overall, you're still moving forward—and at a good pace, we might add.

The stock market is continually priced to offer a positive expected return every day, month, and year. While there is no consistent way to predict when realized performance will be positive or negative, every day the market's expected return exceeds the expected return on cash. Therefore, unless someone can time perfectly when to be in or out of the market, investors will have a higher expected return by staying invested in the market versus moving to cash. To put it another way, when you exit the market, you have, by definition, lowered the expected return on your money.

Again, we can't stress this enough. History has proven that market advances are more frequent, last longer, and have greater magnitude than market declines. This is another reason why most market timing strategies inherently produce a lower return. Now you can better understand why we must depend on data (instruments) and not our own limited orientation (sight and emotions) when it comes to investing.

When is the "best time to invest"?

It's always *right now*.

SUMMARY: Timing the Market

Voltaire famously said, "Common sense is not so common."[9] And if we really stop and consider the evidence, it's common sense that no human being can consistently time the market. In our dynamic capitalist economy, market timing is a fool's errand—whether you try it alone or try to hire someone who claims they can. Market fluctuations simply cannot be predicted nor controlled.

Key Points

- **Why do investors try and time the market?** (1) They have an asymmetric aversion to loss, (2) Wall Street's ability to stoke a Fear of Missing Out (FOMO), and (3) the financial media's extraordinary power of persuasion.
- **Timing methods are failed.** Technical analysis (charting) doesn't work with any consistency. Most timing strategies use data mining, which depends on past information which is no indicator of future success.
- **Real cost of timing is missing the best days.** Missing just the *ten* best days in the market (S&P 500 Index®) over the last thirty years would have reduced actual account values by more than 80 percent versus staying invested for all trading days.

- **When is the best time to get in the market?** Right now. The data is clear. Investors have a higher expected return in the market versus out of the market.

In short, staying invested, regardless of market conditions or undulations, will ultimately provide the return and purchasing-power protection that an investor needs to succeed. Successful investing is not about timing the market. It's about time *in* the market.

If we must be in the markets to win, then how do we pick the winners to invest in?

CHAPTER 3

Don't Play the Market Lottery

"*The lottery is a tax on people who can't do the math.*"[1]

—Sean Kernan

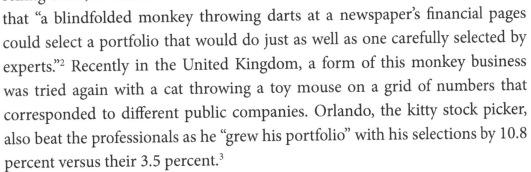

It started in 1973 when Princeton University professor Burton Malkiel claimed in his bestselling book, *A Random Walk Down Wall Street*, that "a blindfolded monkey throwing darts at a newspaper's financial pages could select a portfolio that would do just as well as one carefully selected by experts."[2] Recently in the United Kingdom, a form of this monkey business was tried again with a cat throwing a toy mouse on a grid of numbers that corresponded to different public companies. Orlando, the kitty stock picker, also beat the professionals as he "grew his portfolio" with his selections by 10.8 percent versus their 3.5 percent.[3]

While many brokers and investment managers would admit that timing the market is a fool's errand, almost all of them subscribe to the theory that winning stocks, sectors, or funds can be picked successfully. The fallacy of this assumption is that this means someone else—most everyone else (i.e., the market)—must be wrong. What are the chances of that being the case? This entire picking concept is nothing more than *speculation*. It's not investing.

Let's take a closer look at the concept of stock picking, and why, like market timing, trying to outguess the market is again an exercise in futility.

FUNDAMENTAL ANALYSIS: Fundamentally Flawed

While technical analysis involves using historical data to devise market timing strategies, stock-picking money managers consider themselves *fundamental analysts*.

Fundamental analysts are largely unconcerned with the past price pattern of a stock and believe they can make a definitive distinction between a stock's current price and its true value by pouring over financial numbers to estimate future earnings and dividends. Additionally, various financial ratios and personal interviews conducted with management will supposedly give analysts the tools they need to determine if a buy, sell, or hold recommendation is warranted.

The basic problem with the fundamental analysis approach is the fact that numerous factors are uncontrollable and thus unactionable on a reliable basis. Consider the following:

- **Financial data is historical in nature.** Old numbers have questionable value for predicting the future. Continual revisions make the task even more daunting.
- **Market risk comes into play.** What affects the market as a whole may override any predicted pricing based on the value assessment of one company.
- **Analysts are human.** They may simply fumble an assessment despite accurate data.
- **Consistency is important.** Even if a method is successful once, can analysts be successful again and again—to the extent that they must be in order to populate a properly diversified portfolio? The data overwhelmingly suggest they cannot.

To clarify this last point, consider active mutual-fund managers. They almost certainly will use fundamental analysis to assess the potential buys and sells in their funds. If professional stock pickers are going to tout their skills of selection as their unique ability, they should naturally be willing to stand by their picks down to a relatively short list of positions.

As they look at a group of stocks, the S&P 500 for example (Figure 3.1), they presumably would have the ability to sift this number down to the one hundred best through "careful fundamental analysis" and perhaps a "proprietary selection methodology." But why stop there? Could they not then use the same analysis to pare the group down to the best fifty? What about the best twenty-five of that group? Or even all the way down to the best ten companies in the S&P 500. Would an investor be willing to put all of their money in these ten stocks?

Figure 3.1

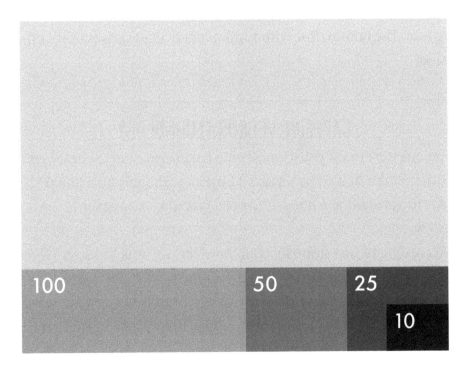

While the mainstream financial media routinely promotes articles such as "The 10 Best Stocks" proclamation, it's rarely made by actual money managers because they prefer to have a larger number of stocks to insulate them against bad picks. This is one reason many mutual funds have identical positions (i.e., stocks or bonds) in their portfolios within the same fund family. We call this fund *overlap*. This duplication of stock positions within a portfolio is in direct opposition to the concept of proper diversification. Yet these money managers will boast of their superior picking acumen.

Unfortunately, when headlines in financial publications make exciting pronouncements, unsuspecting investors take it seriously. Yet picking the best ten out of the thousands of stocks on the exchanges today is an even lower probability than the ten best stocks in the S&P 500 scenario. There are approximately five thousand stocks listed on US exchanges as of 2022. The average US stock fund holds about one hundred stocks.[4] These fund managers are in effect saying that they have picked the top 2 percent of all stocks!

In reality, these writers or managers have no idea what the future holds. "Top 10" articles in financial media have more entertainment value than anything else. The bottom line with fundamental analysis is this: it's fundamentally flawed.

CAFFEINE VERSUS TECHNOLOGY

If someone were to ask you to guess which company had the best performing stock in the first twenty years of the new millennium (2000–2019), which stock would you choose? Apple, Google, or Amazon?

All wrong.

According to Investopedia.com, number one was Monster Beverage Corp. with a twenty-year-trailing total return of 87,560 percent.[5]

Monster is the maker of aggressively branded energy drinks that rose from surprisingly humble beginnings. Before it changed its name to

> Monster Energy, Hansen Natural Corporation started in the 1930s selling fresh fruit juice, eventually expanding to iced tea and natural sodas. In 2002, it launched Monster, "the meanest energy drink on the planet."
>
> Number two during this time period was equally surprising. Tractor Supply Co. is a retail store targeting a very specific market: people who farm as a hobby instead of to make a living. It had a twenty-year-trailing total return of 45,750 percent.[6]
>
> Boring stocks like Hansen Natural and a company with the word "tractor" in it were unlikely stock-picker darlings. But it shows how you never know who the big winners are going to be—and that often the most obvious choices aren't that obvious.

Pickers Can't Even Agree

Figure 3.2 shows the frustrating task investors often face when choosing mutual funds based on ranking services.[7] Observe that these are all respected name-brand companies providing the ratings. They all employ bright people trying to apply their skills to rating funds for investors. But note the disparity among the rankings of these actual funds.

Figure 3.2

	Fund A	Fund B	Fund C	Fund D
*Morningstar**	★★★★★	★★	★★★	★★★★
Forbes	C	A	A+	D
US News & World Report[†]	34	50	10	93
Wall Street Journal	E	C	A	B
Business Week	A	No Rating	B+	C

* Five stars is highest rating; one star is lowest rating   † 100 is highest rating; 1 is lowest

Morningstar and *Business Week* loved Fund A. The other three (*US News* in particular) did not like it at all. Fund B was a favorite of *Forbes* but evidently did not impress anyone else. Fund C was also liked by the analysts at *Forbes* and the *Wall Street Journal*, but no one else (*US News* apparently hated it). Fund D was ranked high by Morningstar and *US News*, but the others rated it as average at best.

If an investor was given this information, which of these funds should they add to their portfolios? Obviously, this range of opinions presents a problem for investors who are relying on the "experts" to help them make selections. The trouble is the rating organizations appear to all use different criteria to make their assessments. So now, rather than just taking their word for it, investors are forced to judge who is using the best standards in their rating methodologies. Even if an advisor or investor were qualified to undertake this task, said methodologies would naturally be proprietary and thus unavailable.

We would submit that we could take almost any actively managed fund in the mutual fund universe and find a similar variety of opinions. This situation as it exists is indeed frustrating for those seeking help. Unfortunately, oftentimes investors simply take the word of only one organization's ratings and move on. This can leave their portfolios vulnerable. The overwhelming majority of mutual fund investors (and their advisors) make their decisions based on this type of confusing ratings information. But there is a better way. Stay tuned.

Tactical Picking

The idea that trying to consistently pick winning stocks is an exercise in futility has been more broadly accepted in recent years. However, a form of picking is still embraced by many, including most investment advisors. Known as *tactical asset allocation*, this idea involves surveying the landscape on different economic levels or categories such as countries, sectors, or asset classes to determine the best place to invest at the moment (more timing).

Shifting all or a part of a portfolio from energy stocks to financials, or from Asia to Europe, or from small to large US companies, are examples. Sounds pretty conventional, right? While this concept certainly can be couched in a way that appears to reflect much consideration and planning, it still smacks of active management, just at a higher level.

The Randomness of Returns

Figure 3.3 shows a list of twenty-two industrialized nations and their returns for a recent twenty-year period.[8] Do you see any trends? Of course not, because returns are random. Yes, there are two three-time winners: Austria and Finland. Also, the United States won the highest return prize only once in 2014, but it was a year in which over three-quarters of the other countries (17) had negative or close to zero returns. What moves can you make in your portfolio with this information? None.

Figure 3.3

THE RANDOMNESS OF RETURNS: COUNTRIES
Annual Return %

	2002	2003	2004	2005	2006	2007	2008	2009	2010	2011	2012	2013	2014	2015	2016	2017	2018	2019	2020	2021
Australia	−1.3	49.5	30.3	16	30.9	28.3	−50.7	76.4	14.5	−11	22.1	4.2	−3.4	−10	11.4	19.9	−12	22.9	8.7	9.4
Austria	16.5	57	**71.5**	24.6	36.5	2.2	−68.4	43.2	9.9	−36.4	25.9	13.4	−29.8	3.5	11.3	**58.3**	−27.4	14.5	−3.3	**41.5**
Belgium	−15	35.3	43.5	9	36.7	−2.7	−66.5	57.5	−0.4	−10.6	**39.6**	27.6	4.1	12.1	−7.6	18.6	−26.9	20.3	−8.1	2.2
Canada	−13.2	54.6	22.2	**28.3**	17.8	29.6	−45.5	56.2	20.5	−12.7	9.1	5.6	1.5	−24.2	**24.6**	16.1	−17.2	27.5	5.3	26
Denmark	−16	49.3	30.8	24.5	38.8	25.6	−47.6	36.6	30.7	−16	31.3	25.2	6.2	**23.4**	−15.8	34.7	−15.4	28.2	**43.7**	19
Finland	−30.3	19.4	6.1	16.7	29.9	**48.7**	−55.2	11.1	10.3	−31.9	14.6	**46**	−0.7	2	−4.7	22.5	**−3.4**	9.5	20.4	9
France	−21.2	40.2	18.5	9.9	34.5	13.2	−43.3	31.8	−4.1	−16.9	21.3	26.3	−9.9	−0.1	4.9	28.7	−12.8	25.7	4.1	19.5
Germany	−33.2	63.8	16.2	9.9	36	35.2	−45.9	25.2	8.4	−18.1	30.9	31.4	−10.4	−1.9	2.8	27.7	−22.2	20.8	11.5	5.3
Hong Kong	−17.8	38.1	25	8.4	30.4	41.2	−51.2	60.2	23.2	−16	28.3	11.1	5.1	−0.5	2.3	36.2	−7.8	10.3	5.8	−3.9
Ireland	−26.2	43.8	43.1	−2.3	46.8	−20.1	−71.9	12.3	−18.1	**13.7**	5.7	41.2	2.3	16.5	−7.1	18.1	−25.3	37.5	15.1	8.5
Italy	−7.3	37.8	32.5	1.9	32.5	6.1	−50	26.6	−15	−23.2	12.5	20.4	−9.5	2.3	−10.5	28.4	−17.8	27.3	1.8	15
Japan	−10.3	35.9	15.9	25.5	6.2	−4.2	**−29.2**	6.3	15.4	−14.3	8.2	27.2	−4	9.6	2.4	24	−12.9	19.6	14.5	1.7
Netherlands	−20.8	28.1	12.2	13.9	31.4	20.6	−48.2	42.3	1.7	−12.1	20.6	31.3	−3.5	1.3	4.8	32.2	−13.1	32.1	24.1	27.6
New Zealand	**24.2**	55.4	35.2	1.7	16.6	8.9	−53.8	50.4	8.3	5.5	29.3	11.3	7.3	−6.3	18.4	11.7	−4	**38.2**	19.9	−17.1
Norway	−7.3	48.1	53.3	24.3	45.1	31.4	−64.2	**87.1**	10.9	−10	18.7	9.4	−22	−15	13.3	28.3	−8.6	10.4	−1.8	22
Portugal	−13.8	43	24.7	−1.9	47.4	24	−52.2	40.4	−11.3	−23.1	3.5	11	−38.2	0.9	3.6	23.8	−11.1	23.7	14.4	0.2
Singapore	−11	37.6	22.3	14.4	46.7	28.4	−47.4	74	22.1	−17.9	31	1.7	3	−17.7	1.4	35.6	−9.4	15	−7.5	5.7
Spain	−15.3	58.5	28.9	4.4	**49.4**	24	−40.6	43.5	−22	−12.3	3	31.3	−4.7	−15.6	−1	27	−16.2	12	−4.8	1.4
Sweden	−30.5	**64.5**	36.3	10.3	43.4	0.6	−49.9	64.2	**33.8**	−16	22	24.5	−7.5	−5	0.6	20.6	−13.7	21.2	23.9	21.9
Switzerland	−10.3	34.1	15	16.3	27.4	5.3	−30.5	25.3	11.8	−6.8	20.4	26.6	−0.1	0.4	−4.9	22.5	−9.1	32.3	11.6	19.3
UK	−15.2	32.1	19.6	7.4	30.6	8.4	−48.3	43.3	8.8	−2.6	15.3	20.7	−5.4	−7.6	−0.1	22.3	−14.2	21	−10.5	18.5
USA	−23.1	28.4	10.1	5.1	14.7	5.4	−37.6	26.3	14.8	1.4	15.3	31.8	**12.7**	0.7	10.9	21.2	−5	30.9	20.7	26.5

highest return of the year

Here we have a real-world (no pun) example of how the random result from previous years provides no advantage or predictability in market performance by country. This strengthens the case for broad diversification across the world-equity markets. Global diversification is vitally important in a superdiversified portfolio. It provides the avenue to share in the prosperity that free markets bring—even at times when the US economy may be lagging.

How Does Socialism Affect Markets?

The Heritage Foundation publishes an annual guide called the *Index of Economic Freedom*.[9] The Index looks at four broad categories with a deeper dive into twelve freedom categories for every country around the globe. They are:

1. **Rule of Law** (property rights, government integrity, judicial effectiveness)
2. **Government Size** (government spending, tax burden, fiscal health)
3. **Regulatory Efficiency** (business freedom, labor freedom, monetary freedom)
4. **Open Markets** (trade freedom, investment freedom, financial freedom)

The Index is intended to provide an objective tool for analyzing a country's political and economic developments. Each of the twelve economic freedoms is graded on a scale of zero to one hundred. A country's overall score is derived by averaging these twelve economic freedoms, with equal weight being given to each.

In order to consider how socialism might affect countries, we looked at the 2022 rankings, which included 177 countries. To give you an idea, the bottom three on the list were:

175. Cuba
176. Venezuela
177. North Korea. (No surprises here.)

The top three were:
1. Singapore
2. Switzerland
3. Ireland

Other notable rankings:
113. Russia
158. China

Consider this: Of the twenty-two countries we considered in Figure 3.3, *fourteen* of them ranked higher than the United States at number 25. A partial list of those that bested the US includes Finland (9), Sweden (11), Norway (14), Canada (15), Germany (16), and the United Kingdom (24). This is hardly a list of countries with what most might consider more conservative governmental systems than ours. We might agree that each of them—along with the others that beat the US—are all more restrictive with their freedoms. Yet, like in the US, the evidence shows that their markets thrive more often than not.

Is this to say that excessive government regulation, loose monetary policy, and more-centralized government authority does not have a negative effect on economies? No. We believe that as these factors are more present, they are more detrimental to free commerce. But it seems that until a deterioration of freedom occurs at extreme levels, as we see in the last three countries on the list, stock markets march on.

What About Economic Sectors?

One of Wall Street's favorite ways to get the attention of investors is picking amongst different *sectors*. Sectors are among the easiest picking strategies to explain and advertise because utilities, energy, consumer staples, etc. are all areas of the economy consumers deal with often, if not every day. Therefore, there is a familiarity with those terms that can create a false sense of comfort to bet on them.

We use the word "bet" quite intentionally here as we often refer to Wall Street as "the House," in much the same way Las Vegas institutions of chance are referred. It's interesting, if not ironic, that the game of roulette has a term known as *sector betting* that allows a gambler to place bets on groups of numbers instead of the traditional 1 in 38 chances of winning.

Just like we saw with the randomness of returns in various countries, the evidence shown in Figure 3.4 testifies to the same unpredictability amongst market sectors.[10]

Figure 3.4

THE RANDOMNESS OF RETURNS: SECTORS
Russell 1000 Index GICS Sectors: Annual Return (%)

	2007	2008	2009	2010	2011	2012	2013	2014	2015	2016	2017	2018	2019	2020	2021
Communications Services	9.24	−32.64	12.39	18.20	4.50	19.49	14.46	2.15	3.47	23.93	−0.91	−14.13	32.46	26.07	18.36
Consumer Discretionary	−11.25	−37.73	45.32	29.97	4.68	24.91	44.58	9.78	7.63	6.66	23.44	−0.93	28.11	47.95	21.67
Consumer Staples	14.18	−16.54	15.59	14.26	14.08	10.57	27.02	16.01	5.67	5.50	12.80	−8.07	26.93	10.78	17.84
Energy	33.68	−36.94	17.11	21.60	3.94	4.44	25.70	−8.62	−22.53	26.38	−1.32	−18.49	10.62	−33.29	55.80
Financials	−17.72	−53.15	15.65	10.69	−19.09	28.92	41.48	12.40	−1.81	21.16	21.61	−13.04	31.79	−1.86	35.67
Health Care	7.81	−23.01	21.47	4.91	11.24	19.41	42.10	25.66	7.23	−2.74	22.27	6.16	21.34	16.81	24.21
Industrials	13.08	−40.84	22.74	26.95	−1.29	16.91	42.10	8.91	−2.95	19.14	21.61	−13.66	30.10	11.96	19.48
Information Technology	16.54	−42.74	62.22	11.17	1.24	14.29	29.90	18.80	5.60	13.10	38.57	0.44	49.67	46.47	30.39
Materials	26.22	−47.31	51.76	24.63	−8.80	16.91	24.28	6.76	−8.76	18.74	24.07	−16.19	24.57	19.37	25.10
REITs	−16.69	−39.11	27.62	28.17	9.74	18.40	0.08	28.50	3.44	6.83	10.02	−3.14	28.34	−5.14	41.56
Utilities	18.87	−29.65	13.14	6.62	19.05	2.03	14.65	27.55	−5.48	17.04	12.29	4.59	25.48	−0.05	17.52
Real Estate	—	—	—	—	—	—	—	—	—	—	30.29	−16.58	39.35	−8.00	44.24

highest return of the year

Even if you could find fund managers who rely on sector bets, the problem for the individual investor is that managers can easily change those bets at will.

These ad hoc allocation adjustments contribute to what is known as *fund drift*. Mutual funds drift away from their original—or stated—investment objectives, which creates portfolio inefficiencies. This means that the portfolio allocation first determined in your financial plan can be superseded without your knowledge or approval by an anonymous money manager thousands of miles away.

What About Asset Classes?

Figure 3.5 provides more of the same evidence as we see the randomness of returns amongst asset classes such as US Large Cap or International Small Cap, similar to what we've seen in countries and sectors.[11] There is no discernible rhyme or reason to why one outperforms another in any given year.

Figure 3.5

THE RANDOMNESS OF RETURNS: ASSET CLASSES
Annual Return (%)

	2007	2008	2009	2010	2011	2012	2013	2014	2015	2016	2017	2018	2019	2020	2021
US Large Cap	5.5	−37.0	26.5	15.1	2.1	16.0	32.4	13.7	1.4	12.0	21.8	−4.4	**31.5**	18.4	28.7
US Large-Cap Value	−0.2	−36.8	19.7	15.5	0.4	17.5	32.5	13.5	−3.8	17.3	13.7	−8.3	26.5	2.8	25.2
US Small Cap	−1.6	−33.8	27.2	26.9	−4.2	16.3	**38.8**	4.9	−4.4	21.3	14.6	−11.0	25.5	**20.0**	14.8
US Small-Cap Value	−9.8	−28.9	20.6	24.5	−5.5	18.1	34.5	4.2	−7.5	**31.7**	7.8	−12.9	22.4	4.6	28.3
US Real Estate	−17.6	−39.2	28.5	**28.1**	9.4	17.1	1.2	**32.0**	4.5	6.7	3.8	−4.2	23.1	−11.2	**45.9**
International Large-Cap Value	7.9	−44.3	37.2	3.8	−10.6	17.8	21.7	−5.6	−8.0	8.0	20.9	−14.5	17.4	−3.1	15.2
International Small Cap	3.6	−47.8	51.4	24.9	−15.5	17.9	26.0	−5.0	**5.8**	4.7	31.5	−17.8	25.9	13.2	11.5
International Small-Cap Value	2.5	−45.6	55.3	21.2	−16.4	**20.1**	28.3	−5.4	1.5	8.4	28.6	−17.9	23.5	3.1	13.8
Emerging Marks	**39.8**	−53.2	**79.0**	19.2	−18.2	18.6	−2.3	−1.8	−14.6	11.6	**37.8**	−14.2	18.9	18.7	−2.2
One-Year US Fixed	5.9	4.7	0.8	0.8	0.6	0.2	0.3	0.2	0.2	0.8	0.6	1.9	2.9	1.8	−0.1
Five-Year US Government Fixed	8.2	**8.8**	0.2	3.7	3.4	0.9	−0.1	1.2	0.9	1.0	0.7	1.5	4.2	4.4	−1.2
Five-Year Global Fixed	6.3	6.6	2.3	2.0	2.3	2.1	0.6	1.9	1.0	1.5	1.1	**2.1**	3.9	3.2	−0.8

highest return of the year

Here is what we can conclude: returns at every level of the market are random, and therefore trying to pick winners is not feasible. In contrast to a tactical allocation, a *strategic* allocation—which ignores so-called tactical market indicators—is the more prudent course.

MARKET ANALYSTS VERSUS METEOROLOGISTS

You may still remember watching the local weather report on one of the three channels of your black-and-white television when the gimmick was for the weather forecaster to come out dressed in garb that coincided with the forecast. A favorite was the ill-fitting raincoat and rain hat. The old joke about predicting the weather and "if you don't like it, hang around—it'll change in an hour or so" is universal. The equipment meteorologists used in those days was archaic by today's Doppler radar, real-time, computerized standards. It's a wonder they ever forecasted correctly. And even today, with all the technology, meteorologists still seem to be incorrect more often than we might expect.

This brings us to the financial market analyst. Each year we see the exercise when all the financial publications and talk shows get the "expert predictions" on how the market will perform. This process also begs the question: is there anyone who can be so wrong so often and still hold a job? And not just any job—one that is well respected and highly compensated! Today's meteorologist looks downright psychic compared to the stock market analyst. Incredibly, however, investors seem to overlook poor financial forecasting as if it never happened.

What short memories investors have! They seem to always be hoping to find that special guru or hot stock tip that will allow their ship to finally come in. This leads to a fundamental problem: investors typically are looking for the short-term fix rather than at the long-term view of their finances. If they were thinking long-term, they would ignore the forecasts. Instead, they would buy and hold superdiversified stock portfolios for the rest of their lives—period. Why? Because there is no better way to create long-term wealth for the average investor.

> Getting in and out based on market events or the analyst-guru's call of the day, week, month, or year is a failed proposition from top to bottom. Free markets work. Capitalism is the economic miracle of history. Get in and stay in.
>
> No rainstorm lasts forever. As long-term investors, we need to keep that in mind. So, when it comes to predicting, give us the weatherman. His short-term forecasts are far more accurate. And his long-term predictions? Well, just like in the market, he says there is always fair weather ahead.

PICKING THE RIGHT MANAGERS: Lottery-Like Odds

Let's say you want to pick good active-fund managers (timers and pickers) in three US stock asset classes: US large cap, mid-cap, and small cap. Assume that an acceptable track record would find the mutual funds of those three managers in the top quartile (top 25 percent) of their fund categories at the end of 2019 (Figure 3.6).[12]

Figure 3.6

Asset Class	Funds
Large-Cap US	175
Mid-Cap US	66
Small-Cap US	122

Next, in Figure 3.7, we see how many active-fund managers finished in the top quartile (25 percent) of their category in the next one-year period of 2020.[13]

Figure 3.7

Asset Class	Funds	Top 25% @ 1 Year	%
Large-Cap US	175	102	58
Mid-Cap US	66	40	61
Small-Cap US	122	69	57

Not bad. You had a better-than-coin-flip chance (50 percent) of choosing a high-performing fund in any one asset class. But the next question we would ask is: "What are the chances that you could pick active managers who finished in the top 25 percent in *all three* asset-class categories for the one-year period?" The calculation is as follows:

$$.58 \times .61 \times .57 = 20.17\%$$
or 1 out of 5

What does this mean? It means that you had a 1 in 5 chance of finding consistently performing (top 25 percent) money managers in each of the three asset classes for the one year following their top 25 percent performance in 2019. It also means you had a 4 in 5 chance of having at least one third of your portfolio lagging the market return. Keep in mind we are looking at the probability of achieving this in just one year. This should seem like a simple task. Yet the evidence shows otherwise.

What about the probability of selecting one of those 2019 "Top 25 percent" mutual-fund managers who would have strung together just two years in a row (2020 and 2021)? Here are the numbers (Figure 3.8). [14]

Figure 3.8

Asset Class	Funds	Top 25% Two Years in a Row	%
Large-Cap US	175	14	6.9
Mid-Cap US	66	1	1.5
Small-Cap US	122	1	0.8

Here's the calculation:

$$.069 \times .015 \times .008 = .000828\%$$
$$\text{or 1 out of 120,773}$$

Maybe you're a fan of the 1994 blockbuster comedy *Dumb and Dumber*. If so, we can imagine you might be thinking of the line, "So you're saying there's a chance..." But realistically, 1 in 116,950 is effectively no chance. And keep in mind, this is a very limited scope analysis. In a full client-portfolio allocation, an investor should use between eight-to-twelve asset classes, and a holding period of multiple *decades*. The trees we would have to chop down to write the full number would be... well, you get it. We are talking LOTTERY-LIKE ODDS here. In fact, you have a much better chance of winning the POWERBALL™ jackpot with a chance of about *1 in 300 million*.

Risk a dollar on a lotto ticket at your local convenience store if you get the urge—but that's no way to manage your nest egg.

SUMMARY: Playing the Market Lottery

Key Points

- **Fundamental analysis is fundamentally flawed.** This primary "tool" for picking stocks depends heavily on human judgment, and therefore human flaws.
- **Pickers can't even agree.** The variety of opinions forces investors to decipher which picking methodology is best. This is an impossible task.
- **Tactical picking is also futile.** Selecting the winning countries, sectors, or asset classes is equally challenging due to the randomness of returns in each of these areas.
- **Picking winning investments is like playing the lottery.** In fact, the odds are more like POWERBALL™.

Investment professionals, who propose stock picking as a winning strategy, are generally very bright people. We believe that many advisors have not been exposed to the evidence that discredits their methods and are honestly trying to do what is in the best interest of investors.

It's also likely, however, that many of them are well aware of the data but are so entangled in the system that provides their livelihood that they simply don't feel they can leave it. Propping up active management is a personal financial decision for many advisors. They must give the illusion that they're doing something (timing or picking) to "earn their keep."

The bottom line is that picking stocks is nothing more than speculation. It's not investing. The number of managers who can successfully pick stocks are fewer than you could expect by chance. Consequently, there's no reason to even play their game.

Yet, for those who can't learn this lesson, a wild goose chase awaits.

CHAPTER 4

Don't Chase Performance

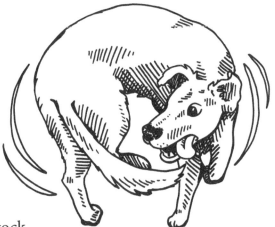

"I can calculate the movement of the stars, but not the madness of men."[1]

—Sir Isaac Newton

Is there a better metaphor for futility than a dog chasing its tail?

We've seen how market timing and stock picking are ineffective and financially unhealthy habits. They are also the gateway that leads to the most futile investing undertaking of all: *chasing returns*. You will soon learn how return chasing is nothing more than "running in circles" only to catch the tail of inferior portfolio returns.

CHASING: Why Do People Do It?

Charles MacKay wrote something almost two centuries ago that helps to explain it. In his book *The Extraordinary Popular Delusions and the Madness of Crowds* (1841), he showed how psychologists had long known that individuals allow themselves to be influenced by a *herd mentality*—or what he called "the madness of crowds."[2] It's a mentality defined by a desire to be like others, to be part of the real "action" or "trend." In the investing world, people think of being part of the "smart money."

But when it comes to investing, "smart" people are not immune to a herd mentality. The hope for large financial profits evokes the human emotions of greed and the avoidance of regret. However, allowing your investment decisions to be influenced by chasing returns can have a dreadful impact on your financial future. Perhaps the greatest example of this phenomenon occurred in northern Europe a great many generations ago.

The Tulip Bubble

Almost four centuries ago, events were put in motion in Holland that led to one of the most spectacular return-chasing, get-rich-quick speculation binges in history.

In 1593, a Venetian botany professor brought a collection of unusual bulbs to Holland from Turkey. Over the next few decades, the tulip became a popular, but expensive, item in Dutch gardens. When the flowers were stricken with a nonfatal virus known as mosaic, it caused colored stripes to develop on the tulip petals. Speculation in tulip bulbs went wild. Popular taste dictated that the more bizarre the bulb, the greater the value.

By 1634, tulip mania had set in. Bulb prices rose out of control. The more expensive the bulbs became, the more people viewed them as smart investments. Traditional industry in the country was dropped in favor of speculation in tulip bulbs. Everyone imagined that the demand for tulips would last forever and that people all over the world would pay any price for them.

People who claimed prices could not possibly go higher watched their friends make enormous profits. The temptation to join them was irresistible, and few Dutchmen sat on the sidelines. In the last years of the tulip craze, people bartered their personal belongings, land, jewels, and furniture to obtain the investment vehicle they thought would make them rich.

As happens in all speculative crazes, tulip prices eventually soared so high that some people decided they should sell. Soon others followed until a snowball effect took over. Panic reigned in no time. The government stated officially that there was no reason for tulip bulbs to fall in price, but no one listened. By February of 1637, less than three years from the beginning of the run-up, tulip dealers went bankrupt, and most bulbs became practically worthless, selling for no more than the price of an onion.[3]

The comparisons that can be made between this historical event and those experienced by so many in modern times are obvious and painful. So how do investors avoid the doom of market bubbles like this? The answer is in the question itself: they become investors and not speculators.

WALL STREET: A Culture of Performance

Former chairman of the Securities and Exchange Commission, Arthur Levitt, refers to the aggressive advertising of past returns as part of the "culture of performance." This suggests a systemic problem that is not easily overcome. Performance is nearly every investor's first criteria. Investment product vendors, knowing this, spare no expense to encourage return chasing in their advertising campaigns.

Their job security and any promotions hinge on the constant attracting of new dollars to their strategies. This leads us to a discussion of the often-manipulative games Wall Street investment firms play. The first one we'll look at is known as *fund incubation*.

Incubator Funds

Have you ever been out to dinner with a brother-in-law who loves to "play the market"? He'll tell you all about his genius decision to invest in a company that just "took off" and made him a fortune. Naturally, "a fortune" is subjective, and he is unlikely to tell you about the dozens of his picks that flopped, right? Wall Street does the same thing, *and* they stick you with the check.

Enter incubator funds.

An incubator-fund strategy works something like this: a mutual-fund company uses its own capital to open several new funds. Let's say they decide on the asset class of US small companies. Each fund would have a different strategy, even if only slightly different. They might rely heavily on market timing, data mining, and picking stocks with various experimental techniques. This is all done "in a laboratory" (albeit with actual dollars) away from public scrutiny.

After each investment strategy runs its course, the odds are that one or more of the experimental funds have hit a random hot streak and shown impressive one- to three-year returns. These survivors can now be marketed and promoted for their high performance. The return-chasing money starts flowing in. And what happens to the losing incubated funds? Their record quietly disappears.

The managers know that whatever stock picking good fortune has come their way will likely not last. So, once they have those incubated higher returns, they can tout them in advertisements and then *migrate to safer stock positions*. This technique may sound a bit fishy. That's because it is. Pretty shrewd of them, isn't it? And by the way, these incubated funds often present investors with higher internal fund expenses due to higher advertising costs and frequent trading. To add insult to injury, it's been reported that *less than half* of the managers in US stock funds own the fund they manage in their personal portfolio.[4] This is more evidence of the misaligned interests that exist between Wall Street's active managers and individual investors.

Another rarely publicized side effect of fund incubation is called *survivorship bias*. Mutual funds that underperform either in the incubation phase or in any subsequent years are swept under the rug like so many dust bunnies.

For example, in 2020 there were 7,636 mutual funds in the United States.[5] But over the previous decade and a half (2005–2020) funds that have closed or merged with other funds numbered 9,714. Naturally, they were usually merged with higher-returning funds. This eliminated almost ten thousand track records that were most likely below average. When these track records are purged, the average returns on all remaining funds go up—thus skewing the average and creating the survivorship bias in the returns that mutual-fund companies are then allowed to report. During this same sixteen-year period, an additional 12,296 new funds were created.[6]

We don't expect this trend to change. The ongoing active survivorship shell game makes it more difficult to get accurate performance information. But now you know—just like the brilliant brother-in-law stock picker—they won't tell you about their failures. So, beware of vanishing funds and the survivorship bias their demise causes.

The DUMB Experiment

We recently decided to go to the archives and blow the dust off some old incubator-fund research Jim did almost twenty years ago.

The experiment was five years in duration and involved "painstaking" research to create a fictitious family of mutual funds. Although there would be no wasted time with stock charting or fundamental analysis, with tongue firmly planted in his cheek, he decided on just one criterion: he simply took all the publicly traded stocks on the US exchanges—from micro-cap to large blue chips—and divided them based on their corporate-headquarters location. So, the initial "incubation" had a hypothetical fund named after each of the fifty states.

For fun, Jim named the fund family the DUMB Funds, or Diversified United States Mutual Fund Balderdash. As you will soon see, this "laboratory experiment" would certainly have been wildly successful in real life.

As shown in Figure 4.1, using actual company return data for US companies, the winner for the first calendar year turned out to be the Wyoming Fund with an incredible one-year performance of 168.2 percent.[7] This was good enough to have beaten every one of the *actual* 2,121 actively managed US mutual funds in the Morningstar universe, no matter how sophisticated their timing and picking strategies.

These phenomenal one-year results would have allowed the advertising of these tremendous results in every major media outlet in the country. The average return of our DUMB Fund family's fifty incubated funds that year was a whopping 74.8 percent. Only one of our funds—Vermont at 22.2 percent—would have trailed the S&P 500 Index®, which returned a very healthy 26.3 percent (not including dividends). Can you imagine the kind of money that would have rolled into the DUMB Fund family with this kind of performance story to tell?

Figure 4.1

DUMB Funds Performance for Year One

Rank	Fund Name	One-Year Annualized	Rank	Fund Name	One-Year Annualized
1	Wyoming	168.22%	26	Michigan	64.10%
2	Oklahoma	156.79%	27	Nevada	61.84%
3	Arizona	147.15%	28	Louisiana	60.93%
4	Colorado	145.18%	29	Connecticut	60.81%
5	Utah	140.44%	30	North Dakota	60.65%
6	Washington	118.33%	31	New Hampshire	59.53%
7	California	109.83%	32	Pennsylvania	59.04%
8	Massachusetts	106.61%	33	Maine	58.81%
9	Georgia	103.73%	34	Arkansas	56.90%
10	Florida	103.41%	35	Iowa	55.50%
11	Minnesota	99.78%	36	Alabama	55.36%
12	Oregon	91.87%	37	Tennessee	50.69%
13	New York	90.48%	38	Wisconsin	48.89%
14	Alaska	87.05%	39	Delaware	47.92%
15	North Carolina	86.37%	40	Nebraska	47.83%
16	Idaho	86.21%	41	Indiana	45.93%
17	New Jersey	84.17%	42	Kansas	45.66%
18	Texas	83.27%	43	West Virginia	45.30%
19	Mississippi	78.40%	44	South Carolina	43.92%
20	Hawaii	77.73%	45	Ohio	43.78%
21	Illinois	71.63%	46	New Mexico	42.91%
22	Maryland	69.73%	47	Missouri	41.15%
23	Virginia	66.37%	48	Montana	30.07%
24	Rhode Island	65.99%	49	South Dakota	29.55%
25	Kentucky	65.93%	50	Vermont	22.21%

As pretend mutual-fund incubators, the next step involved lopping off the bottom ten funds from the list. This brought the average fund return up another 9 percent to 83.8 percent. This is an example of survivorship bias improving fund returns. Just like in actual mutual-fund-incubation strategies, these lower return funds (forty-one through fifty) would be forever invisible to the investing public.

The remaining incredible returns could be advertised for the next two years until another milestone: the three-year returns. Because of the tremendous performance year in which this venture was started, the three-year numbers were almost guaranteed to be superb as well (Figure 4.2).

Figure 4.2

DUMB Funds—Three-Year Performance

Rank	Fund Name	Three-Year Annualized	Rank	Fund Name	Three-Year Annualized
1	Nevada	85.94%	21	Minnesota	21.66%
2	Wyoming	59.31%	22	New York	21.64%
3	Oklahoma	39.07%	23	Maryland	21.17%
4	Delaware	35.67%	24	Rhode Island	20.54%
5	Texas	33.89%	25	Mississippi	20.34%
6	Colorado	32.96%	26	Kentucky	20.23%
7	Alaska	31.83%	27	Virginia	20.15%
8	Arizona	29.79%	28	California	20.01%
9	Tennessee	29.33%	29	Pennsylvania	19.91%
10	North Dakota	29.22%	30	Georgia	19.71%
11	Washington	27.11%	31	Wisconsin	19.66%
12	Connecticut	24.95%	32	Louisiana	19.44%
13	Alabama	24.59%	33	North Carolina	18.89%
14	Arkansas	24.54%	34	Maine	18.66%
15	Illinois	23.91%	35	Iowa	18.63%
16	Massachusetts	23.71%	36	Nebraska	18.44%
17	Hawaii	23.46%	37	Utah	15.60%
18	Idaho	23.02%	38	New Jersey	14.20%
19	Oregon	22.99%	39	Michigan	12.23%
20	Florida	22.60%	40	New Hampshire	5.08%

Of the original fifty funds, the top forty funds had an average three-year annualized return of 25.4 percent. This compared again quite favorably to the most watched of index barometers (the S&P 500 Index®), which returned 14.4 percent for the same three-year period. While beating the S&P 500 by 11 percent was outstanding, why not use the incubation technique yet again to get even more?

The forty remaining funds were simply paired down again to the highest-returning twenty-five. The newly shaded funds in Figure 4.2 were also liquidated from the fund return. This move would have increased the three-year average return of the remaining twenty-five funds to 30.3 percent. Why settle for exceeding a major index benchmark by 11 percent when you can bury them with 16 percent and then promote it like crazy?

At this point, the DUMB Funds could have bought full-page ads in the *Wall Street Journal* and *USA Today* at about $250,000 a pop, for starters. Then their PR director could have easily booked them on all the major financial talking-head programs. What a tour of triumph it would have been, the geniuses of the investing world, and it would only get better.

After the five-year returns came in, the experiment was now going to really pay off. It would be one thing to have one- or three-year averages that looked good. But credibility would be greatly increased if the superior return data could be proven at the five-year mark. Half a decade connotes stability and a perception of a methodology that could work for many years to come.

But not unexpectedly, a regression to the mean occurred as the average for the twenty-five funds shrunk to only 12.6 percent annualized. This would be compared to 12.8 percent for the S&P 500 for the five-year period.

Figure 4.3

Top 10 US Funds Performance for Five Years

Rank	Fund Name	Five-Year Annualized	Rank	Fund Name	Five-Year Annualized
1	Wyoming	31.05%	14	Mississippi	10.45%
2	North Dakota	21.73%	15	Minnesota	10.12%
3	Idaho	20.79%	16	Illinois	9.96%
4	Oklahoma	20.01%	17	Tennessee	9.09%
5	Alaska	18.97%	18	Rhode Island	8.61%
6	Texas	16.03%	19	Arizona	8.23%
7	Nevada	15.84%	20	New York	6.48%
8	Delaware	15.42%	21	Hawaii	6.31%
9	Colorado	13.23%	22	Arkansas	6.13%
10	Connecticut	12.33%	23	Oregon	4.29%
11	Washington	11.54%	24	Florida	3.10%
12	Maryland	11.38%	25	Alaska	2.09%
13	Massachusetts	10.82%			

Uh oh. The jig was up. Or maybe not.

Time for our old friend survivorship bias to enter the scene again. After all this hard work and gathering assets for five years, why let a little thing like a drop in returns undermine the project? It was time to repackage the DUMB Funds and get serious. The bottom fifteen of the twenty-five remaining funds could be eliminated. Then the fund name could be changed and rolled out as the "Top 10 State Funds."

The average return for the Top 10 would be a whopping 18.7 percent per year—almost a full 6 percent higher than the S&P 500. Not only would millions and millions of dollars be gathered based on these five-year published returns, but we would also be able to release the following statement:

> "Five years of intensive research has led us to develop a strategy for selecting the top ten states in the union for your investment dollars. Based on our average annual return approaching 20 percent per year for the group of funds, we believe our methodology has become a proven

way to invest. We expect that these funds will remain open to new investors for at least the remainder of this calendar year and probably until the end of next year."

That last sentence of urgency would capitalize on the FOMO we spoke of earlier and bring in return-chasing money in a hurry. It's also notable that the mutual-fund incubators don't care about the "ones they missed." For example, going back to the DUMB Funds, the South Dakota fund would have ended up at 5 overall with a five-year annual average return of 19.6 percent. But it was removed after the first year because it finished 49 out of 50. This casualty of the process wouldn't have mattered because the fund family managers still would have ended up with what they wanted: returns they could tout as real even though few, if any, investors had likely ever even received them.

It's inevitable that if this experiment carried on, the returns would continue to regress to the mean and get closer and closer to market return. However, in a real-life fund family incubation, the money managers in this experiment would likely have been long gone to another mutual-fund family trying to parlay their "superstar" status and reputation into bigger salaries and higher positions. They're like head college-football coaches who get one Heisman winner or a championship playoff appearance and move on to a ten-year, nine-figure contract.

So, if you see an active manager with superior results in the short run, it's either just plain dumb luck, or it could be the result of an incubator type of strategy. We realize that even after seeing this evidence, some readers may still be tempted to say, "Well, it seems somewhat tricky, but didn't investors get good returns?"

Maybe some did; but for most, probably not.

Let's look at a real-life example of why the vast majority of investors might rarely experience higher early returns.

Funds Prosper, Investors Chase

Figure 4.4 shows the inverse relationship between the assets that are gathered from investors and the performance over a twenty-five-year period in an actual

US large-cap fund.[8] And not just any fund. Peter Lynch is one of only a handful of money managers who might be well-known. He took over as manager to navigate the Fidelity Magellan fund in May 1977, and remained for thirteen years. Between 1977 and 1990, the fund averaged over 29 percent in annual return, making Magellan the best-performing mutual fund in the world.

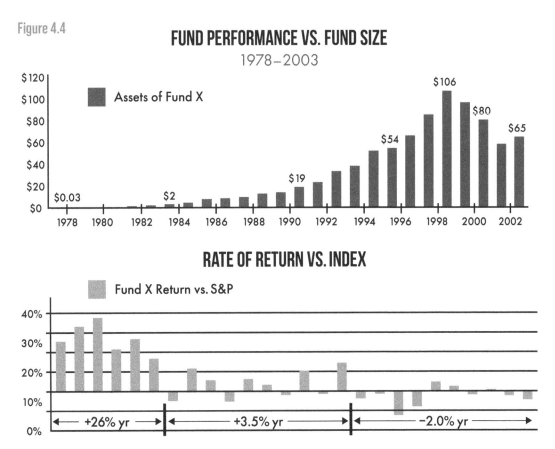

Figure 4.4

By the mid-1990s, the money from investors started flowing in; but by the time the investors began their chasing, the big money was gone and the returns became average at best. From January 1, 2000, the average annual return of Magellan was down −6.18 percent per year (through 2008), trailing the benchmark S&P 500 Index® in six of nine years during that stretch.

Although not shown in Figure 4.4, Fidelity reopened the fund to new investors in January 2008 after a strong year in 2007 when the fund experienced a return of nearly 19 percent. It seemed that the money managers were using the old trick to attract return chasers. In spite of this move, net assets under management continued to fall after the reopening and declined to be about one-third of the 2000 peak—approximately $35 billion by September 30, 2008. Once again, fund families tend to market funds that have done well early.

Again, by the time investors realize the advertised market-beating returns are no longer present, years have passed, and many dollars and opportunities have been lost. This is a clear depiction of how the return-chasing mentality of investors can be preyed upon by the mutual fund industry. And it never stops.

DO YOU ENJOY THOSE SUPER BOWL COMMERCIALS?

One of the most enjoyable aspects of the Super Bowl for many people is the fierce competition among commercials. Who can forget the herding cats, Michael Jordan playing "horse" off tall buildings with Larry Bird, or the historic "1984" commercial by Apple Computer? Each year the ads strive to get more clever, and certainly more expensive. The face ticket price for the game has climbed from just ten dollars for Super Bowl I in 1967 to $1,200 for Super Bowl LVII in 2023. Likewise, a thirty-second commercial in 2023 had a cost of up to an incredible $7 million.[9]

Well, this is fine unless you see your investment company run an ad. If you do, hopefully it will be entertaining, because you just unwittingly helped pay for the most expensive thirty seconds in television. Those advertising costs are passed through to investors—that means you. Worst of all, this expense does little or nothing to benefit current investors but rather benefits the company's effort to recruit new customers. So, enjoy the game. But afterward, you might make a note to check on your mutual fund expense ratios.

The Real Cost of Chasing Returns

Here's a vignette you might enjoy passing along to your kids and grandkids when they reach an age when they want to play the market. (And they all will, by the way.)

> On January 1, 1985, at age twenty-five, Peter Past inherited a $100,000 IRA from his grandfather to invest any way he chose. He decided to look back at the previous year's market results and chose the asset class that reached the highest performance the year prior. How much did this hindsight approach net Paul at the end of the thirty-sixth year (2020)?
>
> He did pretty well. With an average annual return of 6.05 percent, his $100,000 grew to $828,675.
>
> On January 1, 1985, twenty-five-year-old Debbie Diversify also inherited a $100,000 IRA from her grandmother to invest any way she chose. Debbie was not concerned with timing, picking, or chasing the market. She instead held steady with a 100 percent equity Evidence-Based Portfolio.
>
> Debbie earned an average return of 11.8 percent per year, and at the end of the thirty-six-year period, her $100,000 had grown to a whopping $5,545,043.
>
> She accumulated almost *seven times* as many dollars as Peter by simply allowing the free markets to provide what was there for the taking.

This scenario is a microcosm of the return-chasing game investors experience in every generation. Most investors make portfolio decisions just like Peter Past. You now understand that Debbie Diversify knew exactly what she was supposed to do as an investor.

SUMMARY: Chasing Performance

The marketing employed by the active management investment industry entices investors into chasing its best-performing products of *yesterday*. These misaligned interests bring its purveyors profits, while investors usually get only underperformance and frustration.

Henry Blodget, a former stock analyst and Wall Street insider himself, even goes as far as to suggest that actively managed mutual funds should post prominently on their website's cigarette pack-style warning labels that read:

"Active management is hazardous to your wealth." [10]

Key Points

- **Wall Street's "culture of performance" has created investor shell games that can't be won.** Incubator funds, "which lead to survivorship bias," are two of the more damaging aspects that lead investors astray.
- **Mutual fund companies prosper, while investors chase.** By the time the average investor catches up with a money manager that touts a winning record, the returns they hoped for are no longer present.
- **The real cost of chasing leads to mediocrity at best.** Investing in "last year's winners" will predestine a portfolio to underperformance.

We trust these last three chapters have shown beyond any reasonable doubt that active management—timing, picking, and chasing—at its foundation, is a failure. We believe far more money has been lost because of this culprit than all the accounting and trading scandals combined throughout history. At the center is the continued systematic training of Wall Street firm representatives who propagate a flawed philosophy, dooming their clients to investment returns well below what the market offers freely.

In spite of the Wall Street juggernaut, we remain steadfast in our goal to educate as many as are willing to listen about the proper way to invest.

PART II

Evidence-Based Investing

CHAPTER 5

Own the Market

"Divide your portion to seven, or even to eight, for you do not know what misfortune may occur on the earth."[1]
—King Solomon

Congratulations!

You have arrived at the destination of investing made simple, logical, and worry-free. We believe the next hour will be the most impactful of your investment life as we show you the keys to the *only* investment strategy you will ever need.

These foundational money-management tenets will finally put to rest the guesswork that likely has dominated your investment experience up to this point. You're now done with the Wall Street "latest and greatest secrets," as we continue to present the evidence that will provide the peace of mind you long for and deserve when it comes to doing the right thing with your hard-earned nest egg.

So, if you're ready, let's get to work!

We know that portfolio diversification is likely not an unfamiliar concept to you. You're familiar with the old country saying, "Don't put all your eggs in one basket" because when your basket is dropped, every egg is compromised. The trouble is, this is where most investors miss the mark—often badly. They think they are properly diversified, but in reality, they are not.

The term we use is *superdiversification*. This term speaks to the high degree of diversification that occurs when thousands of securities (i.e., stocks and bonds) are combined to provide broad and deep representation of the capital markets. In other words, *own* the market—the entire market.

We'll have plenty more to say about this most important investing concept, but the fundamental idea of diversification in the investing realm is a broadening or spreading out of risk in a portfolio. The simplest way to understand what effective diversification entails is to describe what poor or ineffective diversification looks like.

Imagine looking up at a clear blue fall sky on a Saturday morning. You hear a roar that you recognize. The Blue Angels are practicing. This flight demonstration squadron of the United States Navy can only be described as awesome. Their showcasing of the teamwork and professionalism at the highest level is a sight to behold for proud Americans.

They also provide the perfect metaphor for bad diversification.

We call it the Blue Angel Syndrome. This occurs when portfolios hold similar investments that tend to grow and retreat at the same pace as seen in Figure 5.1. While it's a thing of precision beauty with Boeing F/A-18 Super Hornets, this situation is problematic in the investment world. If everything in your portfolio goes up and down together, you are not diversified!

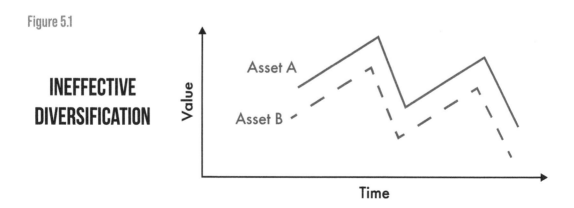

Figure 5.1

INEFFECTIVE DIVERSIFICATION

PROPER DIVERSIFICATION: Made Simple

Conversely, Nobel Prize-winning economist Harry Markowitz's theory of investing showed that to the extent securities in a portfolio do not move in concert with each other, their individual risks are effectively diversified away (Figure 5.2). Proper diversification can reduce extreme price fluctuations, thus smoothing out returns.

In fact, we go so far as to say that if you don't have at least one or two asset-class categories down at all times in your portfolio, then you're not properly diversified and headed for trouble at some point. Yet uninformed investors get anxious whenever they see even one investment in their portfolio underperforming.

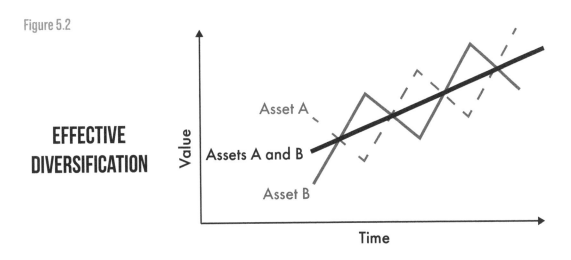

Figure 5.2

EFFECTIVE DIVERSIFICATION

Consider this example. Let's say from January 2002 to January 2022, ABC Company stock rises exactly 15 percent each year. The *standard deviation*—a term referring to volatility—of ABC's returns is zero since there is no variance in this perfectly consistent return. During the same period, XYZ Company stock also averages 15 percent return per year. However, it does so with significant volatility; it has alternating returns of +35 percent and −5 percent. Will ABC and XYZ finish the twenty-year period with the same compounded rate of return?

You're likely ahead of us already. The answer is no. Even though they both have an *average* return of 15 percent, the volatility of XYZ Company stock has cost investors dearly by the end of the twentieth year. Figure 5.3 shows the changes to both investment accounts, assuming a $10,000 investment in each stock.

Figure 5.3

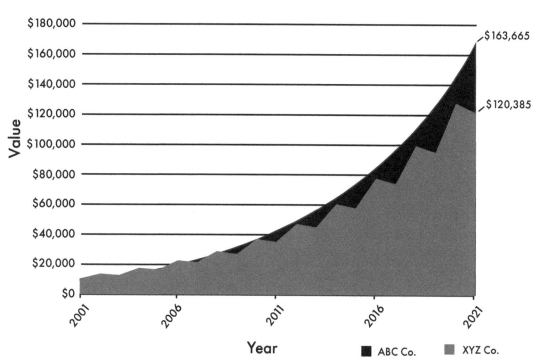

The high volatility of XYZ stock has cost its investors $43,280 over this twenty-year period, which amounts to over one-third more actual dollars in the ABC Co. portfolio. The compound return of ABC stock is 15 percent per year, but the XYZ stock only compounds at 13.25 percent. The higher volatility of XYZ stock has created a lower compounded rate of return. Proper diversification helps mitigate this issue by lowering the *combined* volatility in a portfolio.

THE DOWNSIDE OF YOUR COMPANY STOCK

A common investor mistake involves owning stock in the company you work for. There is a certain loyalty and affection for the brand employees are helping to build, and their familiarity makes it a natural investment move. This *familiarity bias* comes into play in 401(k) plans that hold too much company stock.

Another psychological factor with your company stock is known as the *endowment effect*. It's defined as when an individual places a higher value on an object or investment they already own than they would if they did not own it. This is also a common issue, for example, when we put our primary home on the market. The emotional attachment may create a needed discussion with a realtor to arrive at a "market" price.

In the case of company stock that is not held in a retirement account, there is also a motivation to avoid large capital-gains tax bills that might occur when the stock is sold. This is understandable. One memorable case we encountered involved an executive with a brand-name express mail service who came seeking help with his concentrated (undiversified) position. He had close to $12 million—almost 90 percent of his net worth—tied up in his employer's stock because of stock options he had accumulated up to his pending retirement. Because of the taxes due on the sale, he refused to diversify immediately. He eventually sold the stock at a 60 percent discounted value from its peak. And he still had to pay taxes (although they were much less). It was an unfortunate and unnecessary risk to take.

It's a good saying to invest by: "You must have laser focus to *become* wealthy; but to *stay* wealthy, you must diversify."

It's obvious one stock—or even ten, twenty, or thirty—cannot provide superdiversification. How many do you need? The answer: *thousands*. Spreading that risk all over the globe reduces risk significantly. While the US market is still the largest equity market, its relative size has decreased compared with the world equity market as a whole.

Figure 5.4

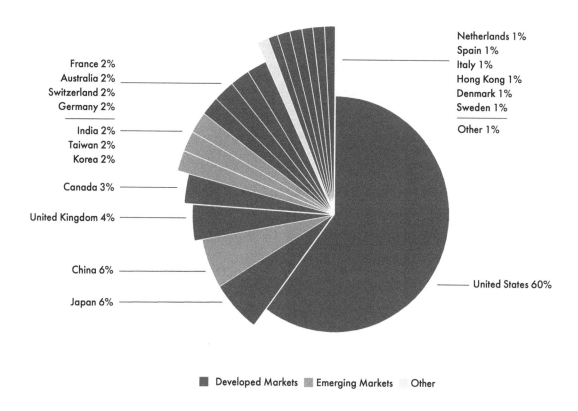

For example, in 1970 the international equity market represented only 32 percent of total world equities. In 2021, non-US markets made up 40 percent of total world equities (Figure 5.4).[2] Consequently, there is a tremendous opportunity to enhance diversification in your portfolio via international markets. Which ones should you pick? Let's use what we talked about in Chapter 3, shall we?

First, on a macro level, Figure 5.5 shows the relative performance of US stocks and foreign stocks from January 1975 to March 2022.[3]

Figure 5.5

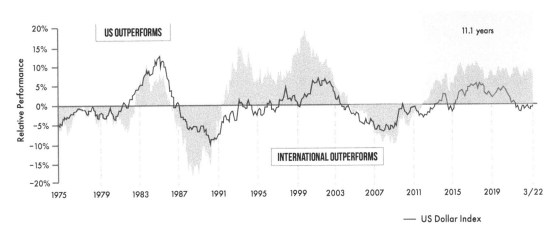

The value of diversification at this level is obvious, as there are long periods when US stock markets either outperform or underperform international markets. By diversifying globally and allocating, on average, 30 to 35 percent of your portfolio's stock allocation in international markets, you can protect your portfolio from downturns and profit from countries that are doing well.

Now you may be tempted to start thinking, "Mmm . . . *which* countries will be the winners where I can load up on their companies?" Not so fast, my friend. You should know better! But we are nothing if not charitable. Please go back and review Figure 3.3 just to make sure you stay on the straight and narrow.

Next, let's talk about the building blocks used to create superdiversification.

EBI BUILDING BLOCKS: Asset Classes

Perhaps you're familiar with the Bible story of the wise man who built his house upon solid rock. The rain came down, the streams rose, and the winds blew and beat against that house, but it did not fall because it had a firm foundation. Conversely, the foolish man built his house on sand. When the rain came down, the streams rose, and the winds blew and beat against that house; it fell with a great crash.[4]

In the financial realm, building a portfolio using active management by timing the market and picking "winning" securities is tantamount to building a house upon the sand that will cause it to eventually collapse. Conversely, an Evidence-Based Investing strategy involves building your investment house upon the bedrock economic system of free capital markets.

So, what are the building blocks of a successful EBI portfolio? They are *asset classes*. An asset class is defined as:

> A grouping of investments that exhibit similar characteristics and are subject to the same laws and regulations.

You may recall that we mentioned asset classes briefly in Chapter 3 when we showed the randomness of asset class returns (Figure 3.5). Let's examine the various asset-class categories.

Asset-Class Categories

Figure 5.6 shows a list of general asset-class categories along with their risk levels. Keep in mind that *risk* in the investing realm does not necessarily have a negative connotation, but rather is a measurement that helps to define the variation in returns.

Figure 5.6

HIGHER ↑↓	Emerging markets
	Small international
	Small US
	Large international
	Large US
	Real estate-investment trusts
	Long-term bonds
	Intermediate bonds
LOWER	Short-term bonds

An EBI portfolio contains a certain allocation to most of these asset classes that are on all parts of the scale. It's counterintuitive to think that by having a portfolio that holds substantial amounts of the higher-risk asset classes that it would have a lower standard deviation. Combining asset classes with *different* risk characteristics actually *reduces* overall risk in a portfolio. This is witness again to the effectiveness of superdiversification.

The risk of the whole is *less than* the risk of the sum of its parts.

We consider this self-evident and is one of the most important points to make about superdiversification and the EBI strategy. We'll provide an example of this in greater detail shortly.

Fool's Gold

On a daily basis, we hear commercials on radio and television that proclaim through their celebrity spokespersons, "gold has never gone to zero." In other words, "Invest with us, and we won't lose it." They play on fear.

In March of 2022, we noticed another ad was repeated often in prime time that had a split screen of four supposed experts saying, "I believe it's the right time for gold!" We happened to notice that there was fine print on the screen showing that this interview took place, in one case, on June 12, 2020. That's almost two years prior to this "right time." They play on greed.

Cable news networks are in the business of attracting viewers to sell advertising. Bad news attracts. Gold trends up with bad political and economic news. Networks then load up with gold commercials. See the connections?

But let's suppose in a weak moment you succumb to the propaganda and want to own some physical gold. First, as a practical matter, it's quite expensive when you consider transaction costs (as much as a 5 percent) and then add shipping costs (gold is heavy). The next consideration is the cumbersome task to store it in a secure location. Do you get a half-ton safe to put in your closet next to your sneakers? Or do you take them to a safety deposit box at your local bank with the added rental cost and inconvenience associated with banking hours?

And while we're hesitant to go apocalyptic on you, wouldn't you feel a bit paranoid in line at the grocery store paying for groceries with a single $5,000 gold ducat? Will they give you change in rice and beans? You also might want to keep your head on a swivel as you walk to the parking lot. (We can't say at this point what might happen to the value or legality of physical gold if our currency becomes digitized.)

So, how has the "oldest, most trusted asset . . . that will never go to zero" performed versus the stock market? If you invested $1,000 on January 1, 1926, and held it through December 31, 2021, here is the inflation-adjusted (if in a tax-free account) amount you would have:
- $1,000 invested in the US stock market would now be worth **$910,000**.
- $1,000 invested in gold would now be worth **$5,730.**

That's almost $1 million, or over 158 times more purchasing power for stocks versus about $6,000 to get a nice safe to keep your future gold in. It bothers us greatly that gold and other precious metals are even touted as "investments" in the first place. An ounce of gold neither produces anything, nor does it make a profit. (What about crypto, you may ask? It's the same in this regard as gold or any other currency trading; it's a purely speculative instrument that has no future cashflows.)

On the other hand, think about what you're doing when you invest in a public company's stock. Before they're worthy of being listed on an exchange, a company has produced great products and services to such a level that they caught the eye of investment bankers who took them public. No easy task. And most importantly, stocks inherently have future-earnings potential that you can share in.

The Golden Question is this: would you rather own the goose, or the golden egg?

Asset-Class Investing

The concept for asset-class investing was born out of Modern Portfolio Theory (MPT). The theoretical foundation for MPT was published by Harry Markowitz in 1952.[5] Along with two associates, Markowitz won the Nobel Prize in economics in 1990 for his work on the subject. Other academicians naturally gravitated to this logical process.

Multibillion-dollar institutional investors—such as foundations, pension plans, and university scholarship funds—have used Modern Portfolio Theory and asset-class investing for decades. This is notable given their fiduciary responsibility. For this reason, these investment building blocks are often referred to as "institutional" asset-class mutual funds. Independent registered investment advisors (RIAs) can provide these same investments for your portfolio in the preservation of capital and its steady, long-term growth.

As the name implies, asset-class mutual funds are designed to deliver the investment results of an entire asset class—such as "large US value" stocks or "small international." We believe that the characteristics of these asset-class funds are best suited to create efficient portfolios that methodically provide portfolio superdiversification.

How Asset Class Funds Are Made

If you were to visit our office in Bryan, Texas, we might show you into our coffee shop where you would see—among others things—a particular piece of sports art. We love college football, but the drawing you think you see there is not a drawing at all. The immensely talented artist used a technique known as *reduction* and actually erased this while observing a photographic image. Yes, that's right. He started with a black background of charcoal and then used an eraser as the tool of trade to "draw" the image.[6] We provided a zoomed in view to show the detail involved. It's even more impressive to see the whole thing in person. So, what does this have to do with investing?

Figure 5.7

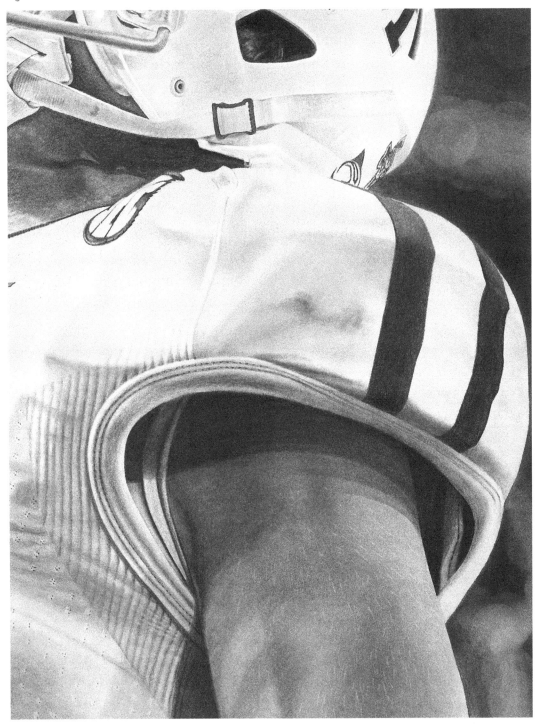

That's how asset-class mutual funds are created. Instead of trying to pick winners, they deselect—or "erase"—unqualified securities.

Institutional asset-class funds use what we refer to as portfolio filters when determining which securities should be held in a particular fund. Generally, this methodology is designed to *eliminate* candidate securities rather than *select* candidates as active managers do. (That's why we call active managers stock *pickers*.)

This subtle, yet critical, difference is the foundation of the asset-class building blocks used in EBI portfolios. It's the key ingredient that eliminates the human element in money management. By using objective-filtering criteria instead of subjective human judgement, the consistency of the EBI-Portfolio approach to investing can be achieved. The following filter chart (Figure 5.8) is a sample of how a US small-cap, asset-class committee might create a fund.

Figure 5.8

US Small Cap—Initial Universe	5,120
Reason for not buying at this time:	
Asset class concerns	−503
Foreign stocks, ADRs, REITs	
Pricing concerns	−169
Recent IPO, financial difficulty, in bankruptcy	
Merger/tender or corporate action	
Trading concerns	−260
Not enough market makers, listing requirements	
Limited operating history	
Miscellaneous	−844
Investment companies, limited partnerships	
Under consideration, inadequate data, miscellaneous	
Total number dropped	(1,776)
Current buy list	3,344

In this example, we see 5,120 securities that qualify as "small cap" (small companies) in the asset-class universe. Each filter would present a reason not to hold a particular security at this time.

Notice that the first reason indicates asset-class concerns. Perhaps the securities are actually foreign stocks or American Depository Receipts (ADRs), which would not qualify as domestic stocks. Or perhaps there are real estate-investment trusts (a.k.a. REITs)—which are companies that own, operate, and finance income-generating real estate. They would have their own separate REIT asset-class fund. You can see that over five hundred companies were "erased"—or filtered out—for these reasons.

The next category would be pricing concerns. Perhaps they are an Initial Public Offering (IPO) in the process of merging with or acquiring other companies, or having financial difficulty. These are all reasons to defer their inclusion in the fund. You can see that 169 were dropped out for these reasons.

Trading concerns such as a limited operating history would cause securities to fall out of consideration as well. In this example, 260 were eliminated for this reason.

Other miscellaneous reasons—such as inadequate data, the fact that the companies in consideration are investment companies, or limited partnerships—could also eliminate them as candidates at this time. A total of 844 were eliminated for this reason in this example.

In all, 1,776 securities were filtered out, leaving 3,344 companies intact. This large number of individual securities shows why institutional asset-class funds tend to provide the purest asset-class representation and superdiversification possible.

In summary, here are five important characteristics of institutional asset-class mutual funds:

1. **Lower costs.** All mutual funds have operating expenses. These expenses are expressed as a percentage of assets and include management fees, administrative charges, and custodial fees. The average annual expense ratio for all actively managed retail-equity mutual funds was around

0.63 percent in 2019. By comparison, the same expense ratio for filtered funds (of which institutional asset-class funds could be considered) averaged around 0.13 percent.[7] They are also 100 percent liquid at all times.

2. **Reduced turnover.** According to a recent Morningstar analysis, the average turnover ratio for managed domestic-stock funds was 63 percent.[8] This high turnover means that if a fund holds one hundred securities at the beginning of the year, at the end of the year, almost two-thirds of them would have been sold and perhaps even repurchased. This is because they attempt to add performance by trading often within a fund (timing, picking, and chasing). It wouldn't be unusual to see an actively managed mutual fund exceed 100 percent turnover in a calendar year.

   By contrast, institutional asset-class mutual funds have much lower turnover rates because of the objective portfolio filters to determine holdings. This keeps costs low, which in turn improves performance.

3. **Tax efficiency.** Mutual funds are required to distribute 95 percent of their taxable income each year to remain tax-exempt. These taxable distributions can have a negative effect on the investor's rate of return. The frequent trading that is used in actively managed funds often results in high turnover and higher tax distributions. Asset-class funds, on the other hand, hold their positions based on structured criteria which leads to lower turnover and greater tax efficiency for investors.

4. **Consistent portfolio allocation.** The largest determinant of portfolio performance is asset allocation. Efficient asset allocation is accomplished when the mutual funds in your portfolio maintain their allocation integrity.

   Unfortunately, return-chasing managers often make random changes to their fund asset-class percentages over time. In addition, they often must sell for cash flow requirements born out of emotional investor overreactions. These ad hoc allocation adjustments create a negative situation known as *fund drift*. This can result in significant change to the composition of a portfolio over time.

Asset-class funds tend to always keep their allocation in their assigned asset class. This allows investors to maintain the Investment Policy Statement (IPS) integrity contained in their financial plan.

5. **Commodity exposure.** Commodities such as precious metals, oil and gas, or agricultural goods can serve as an inflation hedge and provide a diversification benefit in short periods of time. However, this hedge can often come with high volatility. Given this, you run the unnecessary risk of experiencing a big short-term loss using commodities as an inflation hedge. This may offset any potential benefit.

With asset-class funds, there is no need for a concentrated commodity portfolio because they maintain significant commodity exposure through companies involved in energy, mining, agriculture, natural resources, and refined products. This provides essentially a built-in inflation hedge to a large degree.

SUMMARY: Implementing Superdiversification

King Solomon reigned as the purported wisest and wealthiest man who ever lived. Given this, it's not surprising that he knew something about proper diversification. (The opening quote of this chapter was taken from his writings contained in scripture in Ecclesiastes 11:2.)

During his reign (967–927 BC), he became one of the undoubted masters of the Mediterranean Sea and persuaded several other kings to join him in large-scale trading with heavy cargo ships. These fleets returned with fabulous riches. It's easy to conclude that his thoughts on diversification were born out of experience with occasional difficulties such as storms, pirates, or mechanical breakdowns on various voyages. His wisdom to spread the risk amongst multiple ships informs us as investors even some 3,000 years later.[9]

While Wall Street and its allied advisors continue to tout their picking and timing "prowess," we know from the evidence that thousands of positions are required in a portfolio to adequately mitigate unsystematic risk that individual stocks characteristically harbor. In addition, while the ups and downs of the general economy and markets can affect the daily balance of any portfolio due to systematic or "market risk," superdiversification provides broad exposure to both US and international markets to take advantage of the opportunities for long-term growth that free markets have so generously provided.

Key Points

- ***Superdiversification* takes the advantages of conventional diversification to a higher level.** The deep representation of capital markets mitigates the big and all-too-common risk of overconcentration in both stocks and bonds.
- **The building blocks of superdiversification are asset-class mutual funds.** Rather than "picking the winners," they use a deselection process designed to help remove human foibles from the investing process.
- **Gold, precious metals, and crypto currency are not viable investments.** Real investments produce *something*—like company profits and appreciation through owning their stock, or interest payments through bonds.

A successful investment experience is not dependent on outperforming the market. Rather, it's about optimizing your returns in order to achieve your goals. In our next chapter, we will show you the specific optimizers of an Evidence-Based portfolio.

CHAPTER 6

Optimize Your Returns

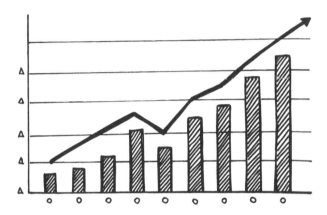

"A wise person does at once, what a fool does at last."[1]

—Lord Acton

When it comes to investing, conventional thinking maintains, "Maximizing returns is the ultimate goal. The higher, the better." If we may, we'd like to adjust that paradigm just a bit and suggest that what investors should really be looking for is to optimize their return while protecting purchasing power. There is a significant difference.

Maximizing attempts to capture the greatest gains possible without regard for the amount of risk taken to obtain them. This can create significant and unnecessary volatility.

Optimizing focuses on investing in the areas that have consistently rewarded investors with higher risk-adjusted returns.

How is this done specifically?

First, we'll examine stocks (equities). As you'll see, stocks are relied on primarily for growth in a portfolio. We will then take a look at *bonds*, or fixed income investments, which play the role of providing more stability and liquidity in your investment strategy.

STOCKS: OPTIMIZING RETURNS

Decades of academic research have identified four areas of optimization that have consistently resulted in higher expected returns over time (Figure 6.1). They are:

Figure 6.1

THE MARKET: Stocks Versus Bonds

This may be obvious to most investors, but the stock market has a greater expected return than the bond market. This is why we constantly remind our own clients that owning stocks is the key to protecting their purchasing power. We refer to this greater average return as a *premium*. Figure 6.2 shows the annual compound rate of return of four broad asset classes over the last ninety-five years:[2]

Figure 6.2

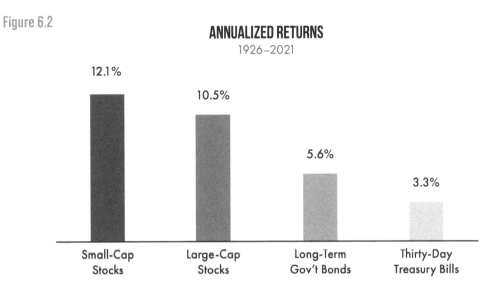

Notice that the average annualized return of bonds is well under *half* that of stocks. The owners of stocks have clearly had the advantage in the long run. Figure 6.3 further confirms a substantial advantage (premium) of +8.65 percent annualized that the US stock market has over one-month treasury bills.[3] (One-month treasury bills are generally considered the cash equivalent in comparison studies.)

Figure 6.3

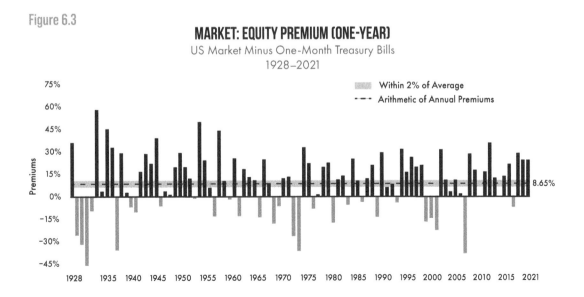

Next, when we consider the higher ordinary-tax rates of bond interest (currently as high as 37 percent in the top bracket) versus the long-term capital gains treatment available in equities (20 percent or even 0 to 15 percent at lower income levels), we have the makings of an even larger gap as stocks outpace bonds by a roughly 3 to 1. In Figure 6.4, we show the returns after the highest tax brackets have been applied.[4]

Figure 6.4

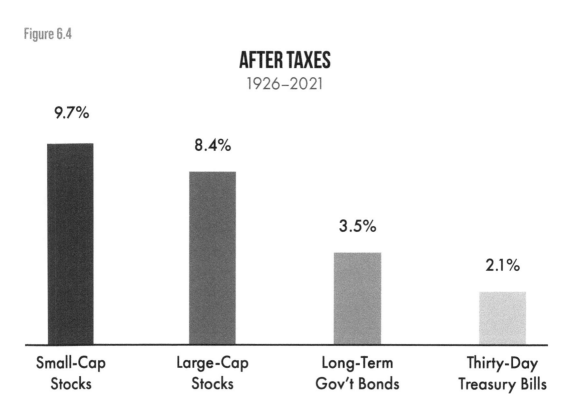

Finally, when inflation is taken into consideration, the gap widens even further. Even though inflation has averaged only about 3 percent during this extended period, the return multiple for stocks changes dramatically as bonds provide little or no growth after taxes and inflation are considered (Figure 6.5).[5]

Figure 6.5

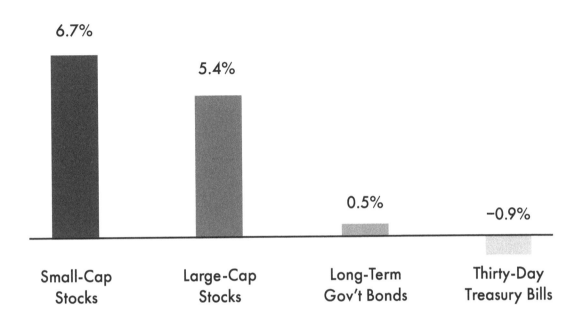

Are Stocks Actually Safer Than Bonds?

At first glance, this looks like a strange question. Obviously, bonds have lower risk from the standpoint of less price fluctuation (standard deviation), and therefore, are significantly "safer" in the conventional sense—at least in the short run. For this reason, they can serve an important purpose in a portfolio to dampen volatility and provide cash flow liquidity when needed.

But our investing life is never a sprint.

The prudent investor understands that the race is a marathon, and during the race, you must occasionally bear some downward fluctuations in your portfolio value. It's the *investing law of gravity*. If you demand only safety of principal, then you are doomed to receive low returns. But given that one of the biggest enemies to long-term investment success is inflation, stocks are by far the most effective and efficient tools to use to overcome its insidious effects. Remember: it's not about protecting only principal; it's about protecting *purchasing power*.

> Bonds: short term, reliable; long term, uncertain.
> Stocks: short term, uncertain; long term, reliable.

The Inflation Challenge

There is no more destructive force to an economy, or even to a society, than runaway inflation. In our office, we have a framed reminder of that destruction in the form of a billion-mark German bank note from 1923 (Figure 6.6). It's printed on only one side because so many notes were needed in such a short time that printers could not keep up. One billion marks, by the end of 1923, would not even buy a loaf of bread, and eventually one US dollar could buy 2.5 trillion marks.

Figure 6.6

The inflation rate is a useful gauge of an economy's health. When it's healthy, businesses become more productive, consumers spend freely, and supply and demand (supply chains) are in equilibrium. When inflation is steady at around 2 percent, the economy is more or less as stable as it can get.

Will we ever see one-sided greenbacks with this kind of devastation to our purchasing power in America? Hopefully not. But that doesn't mean that inflation can't be abnormally high compared to what we've seen in the US for the last thirty years. Investors must be vigilant. There is a definite advantage to holding stocks versus bonds when the effects of inflation and taxes are brought to bear on a long-term portfolio.

COMPANY SIZE: Small Versus Large

The second area of optimization we can observe is based on company size. In Figure 6.7, we see the black bars above the midline, which shows the years when small "caps" (small public companies on the stock exchange) beat large-cap companies.[6] The gray bars below the midline indicate when, on average, small companies underperformed large companies.

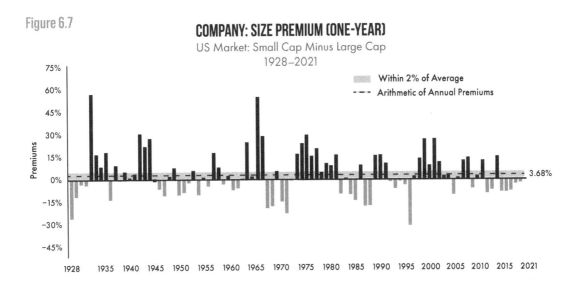

Figure 6.7

The annual small-cap stock returns have varied widely, sometimes experiencing extreme positive or negative performance compared to the large cap. Yet, overall, for almost a century, small-company stocks have substantially outperformed large companies to the tune of about +3.68 percent per year on average. Why have small companies outperformed larger companies?

Small companies tend to be nimbler and can often take advantage of economic events and trends more easily. This, in turn, allows for historically better returns on investment (ROI) than the big guys. The significant upside growth potential might be the primary advantage of small-cap stocks. Merger and acquisition activity tends to be greater as well, which often provides another opportunity for small-cap investors.

While small-cap companies tend toward a higher reward (return) than larger companies, keep in mind that it also comes with a higher degree of risk. This is another reason why superdiversification is key in any investment plan.

RELATIVE PRICE: Value Versus Growth

The third stock optimizer we can empirically observe is based on *relative price*. Another way of referring to this aspect is a more common term of *value* stocks versus *growth* stocks. Value stocks are categorized as having a high book-value-to-market value ratio. This gives a perception that it has a bargain price as investors see the company as unfavorable in the marketplace.

As before, Figure 6.8 shows the black bars above the midline indicate the years when value stocks beat growth stocks. The gray bars below the midline show when value stocks underperformed growth stocks on average. The research has shown repeatedly that, over the long term, value stocks have outperformed growth stocks by an average of +4.22 percent.[7]

Figure 6.8

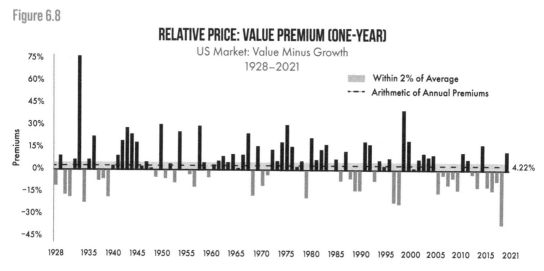

To many investors, selecting value over growth may seem counterintuitive. Most believe that selecting growth stocks would make more sense, especially if that is exactly what they're trying to do: *grow* their portfolios. However, the added risk associated with value companies naturally requires a higher return from investors given the category's higher standard deviation (the measure for risk). Higher risk, higher return.

It's worth mentioning that at press time, the world economy was experiencing an inflationary trend. It's notable that value stocks tend to become more attractive during periods of higher inflation. Looking again at Figure 6.8, this can be seen, for example, during the decade from the mid-1970s to mid-1980s when inflation hovered in the 7-to-9-percent range. To put it another way, historically, inflationary periods are positively correlated with value stocks outperformance. Note that this does not mean value stocks outperform only in inflationary periods, as is shown in the low-interest period from 2000–05. Likewise, investors should not assume that value stocks always outperform during periods of inflation.

PROFITABILITY: High Versus Low

The fourth and final optimizer considers the obvious pursuit of highly profitable companies versus those with low profitability. Figure 6.9 shows an average return premium of just over 3 percent since 1964. It's not unexpected that we would want to own companies that make higher profits. That's always been a chapter in the "Investing 101" textbook.[8]

Figure 6.9

This area is highly data driven and complex. But it boils down to this: what makes a company profitable? Let's look at a simple example.

Suppose an investor wants to purchase some rental property as an investment and is trying to decide between two properties. Property A generates a high rental income but must use the majority of that income to pay for the high maintenance costs of owning that property. Property B also generates a high rental income but incurs much lower costs to maintain the property. Which one is more profitable? While both properties generate high rental income, Property B is obviously more profitable because it allows the investor to put more of the rental income in their pocket.

The same principle applies to stocks, as a 2012 landmark study by Robert Novy-Marx showed.[9] Just because a company makes a lot of money does not mean it is a profitable company for an investor. The costs to generate that revenue must also be considered. Therefore, investors should seek companies that generate high revenue but with lower costs to operate. These typically result in a higher expected return for investors.

This brings up a natural question: why not just find all the profitable companies and only invest in them? As we've seen, there are other factors that optimize a portfolio. Profitability is just one of these contributing to higher expected returns. And it is not necessarily the most significant one.

For EBI investors, all of the areas of optimization must be considered, but this is an area where ever-improving technology has allowed us to have one more factor to increase the chances of having a successful investment experience.

Reviewing the Equity Optimizers

Figure 6.10 brings our discussion together in one visual to show long-term averages for all the optimizers of expected returns. This data offers ample evidence that considering the additional return premium for stocks (versus bonds), company size (small cap versus large cap), relative price (value versus growth), and profitability (higher versus lower) have been persistent factors to consider over time and pervasive across markets. Each return premium has appeared over many decades in the US market. (Looking beyond the US markets, these premiums have also appeared in developed international and emerging markets.)

Figure 6.10

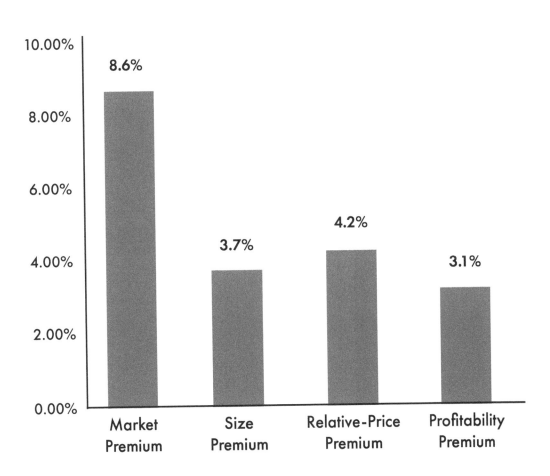

SUMMARY OF OPTIMIZERS OF EXPECTED RETURNS

This evidence should provide you with greater confidence that accepting market risk in stock markets will likely continue to persist in future time periods. Yet you must keep in mind that at every level (individual stocks, countries, sectors, or even asset classes) you never know which parts of the markets will outperform from year to year. By holding a globally superdiversified portfolio across every asset class, investors are positioned to capture returns wherever and whenever they might occur.

BONDS: OPTIMIZING RETURNS

It is rare to see an individual investor hold 100 percent of their portfolio in stocks. Over our careers, the most often used stock-bond mix is a 60 percent stocks and 40 percent bonds. However, please be aware that this strategic allocation between stocks and bonds is a decision to be based on individual investor goals and needs.

On the fixed income (or bond) side of the portfolio equation, we like to keep it simple (Figure 6.11).

Figure 6.11

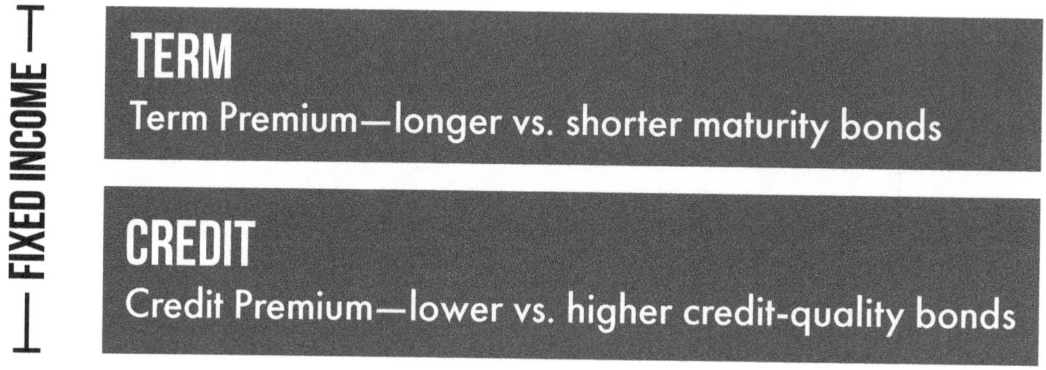

FIXED INCOME

TERM
Term Premium—longer vs. shorter maturity bonds

CREDIT
Credit Premium—lower vs. higher credit-quality bonds

The first optimizer to consider on the fixed-income side of the portfolio is the duration or *term* of the bonds held. Bonds have an inverse relationship to interest rates. Additionally, longer-term bonds entail more risk with diminishing returns. For this reason, the bond asset-class funds used in the construction of an EBI portfolio are primarily short-term in nature (less than five years). As interest rates climb, bond values decline. Likewise, when interest rates decline, bond values rise. Figure 6.12 shows a typical bond risk-return relationship. [10]

Figure 6.12

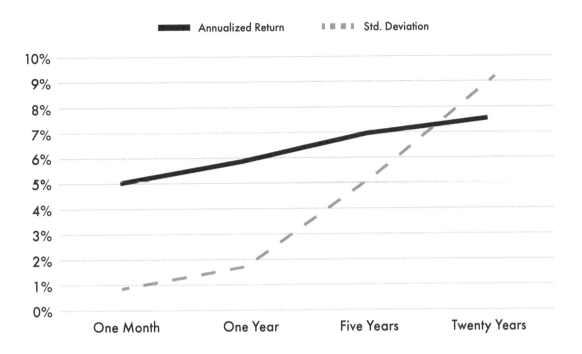

The longer the duration of a bond, the greater the risk, and thus the greater the potential decline. By holding shorter-term bonds, you can reduce the erosion of principal in rising-interest-rate periods. Also, as shorter-term bonds reach their maturity date, they can be renewed at the prevailing higher rate in a rising rate environment.

The second optimizer to consider in the fixed income space is *credit quality*. High quality (AAA and AA) are considered best, given the fact that we are placing the responsibility for the greater portfolio return on the backs of the four optimizers in the stock (equity) markets.

In essence, bond (fixed-income) duties are primarily limited to:
1. Creating greater liquidity and cash flow availability.
2. Mute the high volatility that occurs periodically on the stock side of the portfolio.

We typically include both US and global bond funds to provide further diversification.

EBI PORTFOLIOS: Comparing Allocations

Knowing what you now know about stocks versus bonds, having even a 100 percent stock portfolio should no longer be a scary proposition. However, as mentioned, most investors will ultimately require some fixed income in their retirement years for cash flow purposes and to align with their personal risk tolerance.

Let's consider the following table (Figure 6.13) with six EBI portfolios with different levels of stock exposure in twenty-percentage-point increments. The calculations assume an initial investment of $100,000 in a nontaxable account from 1985–2021.[11]

Figure 6.13

Stock Allocation %	Bond Allocation %	Annualized Return	Total Dollars
100	0	11.8%	$6,199,358
80	20	11.1%	$4,913,831
60	40	10.2%	$3,636,796
40	60	8.8%	$2,266,048
20	80	7.1%	$1,265,349
0	100	5.1%	$629,942

Based on these returns, Figure 6.14 then shows this same thirty-seven-year comparison of account values graphically.

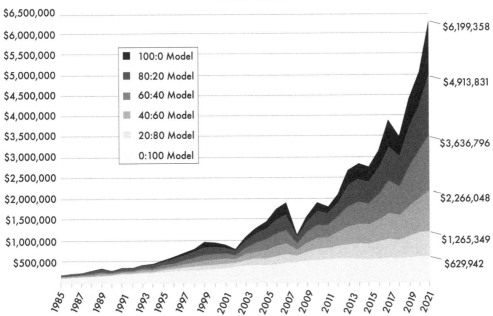

Figure 6.14

Here are the key take aways:

1. The difference between the top (100 percent stocks) and the bottom (100 percent bonds) dollar figures are ten-fold. Certainly a 100 percent bond investor could have avoided short-term stress in their retirement plan because they missed the big market fluctuations. But there are other considerations such as: (a) the *long-term stress* of possibly running out of money in their golden years and depending on adult children for support, and (b) the satisfaction that comes with full self-support and additional opportunities to do meaningful things with more money. This might include leaving a greater financial legacy for loved ones or supporting other worthy causes.

2. The various levels of stock exposure play out in the form of actual results. Figure 6.14 clearly depicts that there is an incremental increase in dollars with each additional amount (+20 percent) invested in equities.

3. While this figure doesn't specifically show this data, we would note that in the thirty-seven-year period depicted, the 0 percent equity/100 percent bond model had *five* years of negative returns. What about the other end of the spectrum? The 100 percent equity/0 percent bonds had only *nine*. This means that, on average, three out of every four years in an *all-stock* portfolio, the yearly return is positive. The 75 percent bull runs hold again. That's not the picture we get if we listen to the fear-mongering financial media and Wall Street, is it?
4. A fallacy of conventional mainstream investing thinking says, "If I take more risk in my portfolio, sure, the highs might be higher, but the lows will also be lower. Therefore, I just can't tolerate that risk." But as you can see in this figure, this is not the case. At least in the long run. Highs are higher for sure, but the lows are *higher* too.

The fourth takeaway is critical to understand, as is evidenced in Figure 6.14 during the 2008 dip where investors who took more risk certainly saw their account values drop more in actual dollars. But where did they end up? The graph shows that if they stayed the course, they still had more money at the end of that deep market downturn with which to build on versus those who opted for less portfolio risk.

SUMMARY: The Optimizers of Returns

Our hope now is that you're beginning to see why we always tell investors that "Evidence-Based Investing changes everything." We ultimately want you to experience a calm concerning the market ups and downs that might have troubled you greatly before. Any worry concerning financial markets can be replaced by the peace of mind that comes from understanding the benefits of an Evidence-Based Investing portfolio and the optimizers of returns in your portfolio.

Key Points

- **Stocks (equities) are "safer" than bonds in the long-term when it comes to protecting *purchasing power*.** They have outperformed bonds (fixed income) consistently and by a wide margin over the long term. This makes stocks the primary hedge against inflation.
- **Small company stocks have historically outperformed large company stocks over the long term.** Small public companies have the advantage of being nimbler as economic events transpire.
- **"Value" companies outperform "growth" companies on average over the long term.** Value companies also tend to perform better in inflationary periods.
- **Bond investments have two purposes.** They help mute market fluctuations and provide liquidity for cash flow when needed. Therefore, they should remain short in duration and high quality. This allows an investor to take properly calculated risks on the stock side of their portfolio.

Next up, if you can't control your emotions concerning your investments, all the guidance we've offered will have been for naught.

CHAPTER 7

Manage Your Emotions

"The hardest victory is over self."[1]
—Aristotle

Siren, in Greek mythology, was a creature half bird and half woman who lured sailors to the rocky shores of destruction by the sweetness of her song. In Homer's *Odyssey*, the Greek hero Odysseus—advised by the sorceress Circe—escaped the danger by stopping the ears of his crew with wax so they were deaf to the Sirens' song. Odysseus had such a desire to hear their song that he had himself tied to the mast. This provided a safeguard against him steering the ship off its course to certain doom amongst the crags from where the Sirens were perched.[2]

This myth practically explains itself when it comes to the investing world as you now know it. It doesn't matter how well you've learned your lessons concerning Evidence-Based Investing if you can't maintain your heading through the market storms and resist the temptation to listen to the "songs" of Wall Street and its compliant media.

MANAGE YOUR EMOTIONS: Especially Fear

Humans are wired to make poor decisions about their money, especially in times of heightened emotion. As we know, Wall Street helps to perpetuate an emotional state of anxiety because they know that fearful investors are compliant investors. They and their media accomplices use even a momentary lapse in investor discipline to foment a wrong sense of market timelines that leads to an *in perpetuity bias*. This bias lulls investors into believing that short-term forecasts are really for the long term. But, as you know, forecasts are inherently short-term in nature. Even then, they are more often wrong than right.

Ironically, one key to a successful investing experience is understanding that we humans are simply not wired for long-term disciplined investing. We're all subject to faulty reasoning. Figure 7.1 shows several of the primary mental errors we make in our investing decisions.

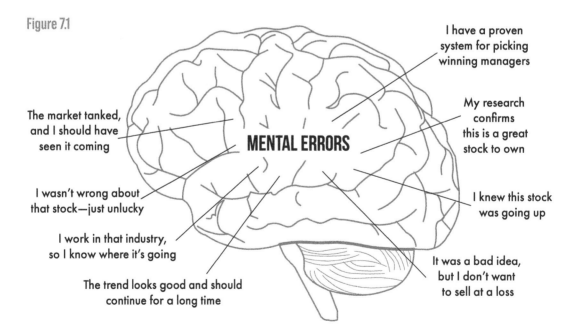

Figure 7.1

There's a seductive component to bad news, and the Wall Street marketers (and their advisors) know it. That's because in the securities markets, progress happens slowly and often goes without notice. But market downturns tend to happen so rapidly that they can't be ignored. The intellectual allure of pessimism has been known for ages. John Stuart Mill wrote in the 1840s:

> "I have observed that not the man who hopes when others despair, but the man who despairs when others hope, is admired by a large class of persons as a sage."[3]

Because pessimism receives such widespread billing and feeds into this "fear factor," investors are susceptible to certain investing traps. Let's take a look at five that are all too common.

1. Fear of Daily Market Swings

What about investors who just can't help checking their phones to see if the day's trading session is green or red? This tri-graph (Figure 7.2) may be the best way to encourage frequent market checkers to break this unhealthy habit and stop worrying about daily market swings.

Figure 7.2

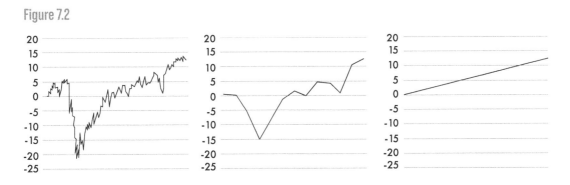

Which of these investing journeys do you prefer? We're guessing the third one, right? In fact, they are all the same one-year journey in 2020. The only difference is the frequency of measurement: daily, monthly, yearly. They are all graphing the S&P 500 Index® return of 18.34 percent from the first trading day in January to the last trading day in December.

Almost any individual year like 2020 can be seen as a microcosm of market behavior. Investors who obsessed over daily numbers could have found many reasons to be pessimistic about market returns as COVID-19 brought uncertainty to all aspects of our lives like never before.

Hopefully they learned one way or another to focus less on daily market changes and more on the long term.

2. Fear of a "Black Swan"

A *black swan* is a term that was popularized by a book by the same title written by Professor Nassim Nicholas Taleb. A black swan is generally defined as *an event that goes beyond conventionally expected events that has potentially severe consequences.*[4]

Taleb describes a black swan as an event that:
1. is so *rare* that even the possibility that it might occur is unknown;
2. has a *catastrophic* impact when it does occur; and
3. is typically explained in *hindsight* as if it were predictable.[5]

The crash of the US housing market during the 2008 Global Financial Crisis is one of the most recent and well-known financial black swan events. The effect of the crash was economically catastrophic on a global scale with no warning. Going back further, the dot-com bubble of 2001 is another black swan event that has similarities to the 2008 financial crisis. Credit crises are classic causes of black swan events.

We intuitively know that things, which have never happened before, happen all the time. Yet, as we've seen throughout this book, free markets are so incredibly resilient that no black swan has been able to overcome them to date.

3. Fear of Another Pandemic

While the COVID-19 pandemic was not a direct economic event, many considered it to be a black swan. Yet pandemics of various sorts have been somewhat frequent in the last half century. Their effects on financial markets have also been well-documented. We looked specifically at COVID-19 earlier when we discussed its regression to the mean after a precipitous drop in March 2020.

It's the same pattern of recovery we've seen historically. As Figure 7.3 shows, epidemics and other health scares have upset markets before. However, in each case, it was only a temporary setback.[6]

Figure 7.3

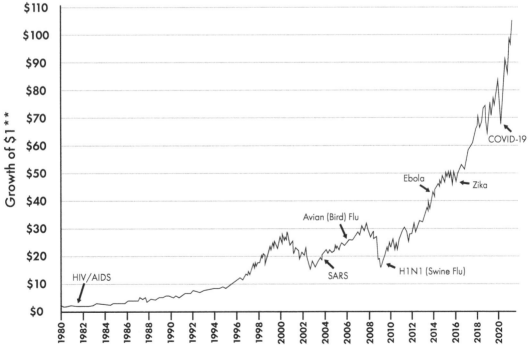

EPIDEMICS AND STOCK MARKET PERFORMANCE
January 1, 1980–March 31, 2021

Epidemic	Date	Following 6 Month Return*	Following 12 Month Return**
HIV/AIDS	June 1981	-3.98%	-12.31%
SARS	Apr 2003	15.53%	22.66%
Avian (Bird) Flu	June 2006	12.68%	20.49%
H1N1 (Swine Flu)	Apr 2009	20.06%	38.78%
Ebola	Mar 2014	6.36%	12.61%
Zika	Jan 2016	13.31%	20.03%
Covid-19	Mar 2020	31.30%	56.33%

*The following six- and twelve-month return is the total return starting the month after the stated date of the epidemic
**The growth of $1 in the IFA SP 500 index is based on total returns

4. Fear of Wars

Marv Levy, the former great head-football coach of the Buffalo Bills, was once asked by a reporter, "Is this game a must win?" He replied, "World War II was a must win."[7] His perspective was wise, and we are a blessed nation to have prevailed in that world-wide threat to freedom.

As conflicts occur across the globe, investors naturally ask, "What effect will this have on the economy and the markets?" and, "Should I make any adjustments to my portfolio?" To gain insight that helps answer these questions, it's helpful to look at the effects that armed conflicts have had through the years. Figure 7.4 shows the annualized returns of two major US-market indices the year a conflict occurred as well as in the following three-year period.[8]

Figure 7.4

Conflict	Time Period	S&P 500	Small US Co.
World War II	1941	-11.58%	-11.00%
	1942–1944	21.96%	40.90%
Korean War	1950	31.74%	39.20%
	1951–1953	13.27%	11.70%
Cuban Missile Crisis	1962	-8.73%	-15.70%
	1963–1965	17.17%	17.30%
Vietnam War	1964	30.55%	17.60%
	1965–1967	6.26%	12.90%
Desert Storm	1991	30.55%	46.40%
	1992–1994	6.26%	22.40%
Iraqi Freedom	2003	28.69%	55.80%
	2004–2006	10.40%	14.60%

First, we can make some general observations. The effects in the year the conflicts began have varied. The stock markets were largely negative in the year World War II began and during the Cuban Missile Crisis but were up considerably the years each of the other four conflicts began. However, it's difficult to draw much of a conclusion from this information given the fact that both WWII and the Cuban incident took place late in their respective calendar years. Second, and perhaps most significant, the average three-year period returns following the year the conflicts started were all positive, with most up significantly.

This data suggests a couple of things: one, it could be argued that the effects of war on the economy were either already factored into the markets or became factored in early in the conflict; and two, while the news from each conflict was at times very bad, it was still only one factor in the world's most powerful economy.

The conflict with Iraq was spawned out of the war on terrorism. In this regard, it's similar to the Cuban Missile Crisis, which was technically not an armed conflict. While the Cold War was at full throttle in 1962, it was also an ocean away and without social media to constantly remind us. The Cuban crisis brought the threat of ending the American way of life within ninety miles of our shore—a wakeup call, to say the least. Yet capital markets rose over the next three-year period (and well beyond).

There are no historical reasons to believe that free markets will do anything other than survive and then thrive after any future conflicts. But we must be willing to protect freedom (and thus free markets) when threatened.

Timing markets based on the latest black swan, geo-political scare, or epidemic drives many investors to do exactly the wrong thing at the wrong time. Overreaction in the spur of the moment almost always results in missing out on any ensuing market rebound.

5. Fear About Presidential Administrations

If we track the S&P 500 Index® back to 1926, we can see in Figure 7.5 how large US companies faired during each presidential term.[9] (Note that when party affiliations are the same for consecutive administrations, the time periods are combined.) Of the seventeen periods shown, only two—Herbert Hoover and George W. Bush—had administrations where the index ended lower at the end of their tenure than where it started.

Figure 7.5

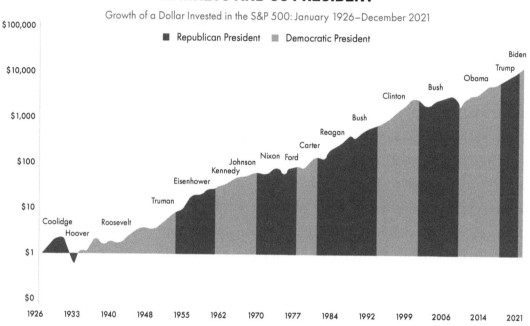

Further evidence at the congressional level makes the case even stronger. For this same ninety-six-year period with twenty-four midterm congressional elections occurring, the S&P 500 Index® (with dividends reinvested) posted an average return of 12.33 percent for all calendar years and true to market form, results were negative in roughly *one out of four*. The average return for the twelve-month period *following* each election was significantly higher at 19.58 percent, with *only one* negative result.

Market timers might use this information as a reason to load up on stocks just prior to every midterm election. Not so fast. Drawing conclusions from so few observations (only twenty-four) is not exactly statistically significant. But if investors are looking for reasons to agonize over election returns, there is little evidence that any changes in political leadership are useful in making portfolio decisions. Citizens may express their opinion at the ballot box once every two years. But as consumers, they convey their opinion every day by where they spend their money.

Government policies may certainly have an effect—either positive or negative—on some firms, but the executives heading up these firms must consider a multiplicity of factors continually. CEOs might be concerned with elections to some degree, but doesn't it make more sense that they are more concerned with the day-to-day overseeing of their vast enterprises?

A healthy representative democracy depends on active voter involvement. But predicting election outcomes is difficult, and predicting how securities markets will react to those outcomes is even more so.

As you can see, there is no definitive data sufficient to make a claim that one party has an advantage over another when it comes to controlling markets. Rather, we believe it's a testament to the resilience of the free market, and its "invisible hand" resulting from the decisions—great and small—that each of its millions of participants have made over the last century. World and political events have a short-term impact on markets but nothing that is actionable for long-term effect.

> ## The Fear Tax
>
> As defined by economists, *opportunity cost* is the loss of potential gain from one alternative when another alternative is chosen. To calculate the opportunity costs involved when choosing when to invest, you must consider how markets generally move and what you would be giving up by keeping money outside the market. We also refer to this concept as the Chicken Little Fear Tax (Figure 7.6).
>
> For an application of this insidious form of "taxation," we need look no further back than March 11, 2020, and the extraordinary circumstances

that led to a rapid drop in stocks at the outset of the COVID-19 pandemic. The S&P 500 Index® dropped −18.38 percent within just nine trading days (March 11–23, 2020). A scary time for all. Yet, what followed was a raging bull market that saw gains of +66.8 percent by the end of the year (March 23, 2020, to December 30, 2020). Furthermore, the S&P 500 grew to a new all-time high of 4,704.54 on November 18, 2020, resulting in a +110.27 percent jump from the March 23, 2020, bottom.

To fully appreciate the opportunity cost of this situation, let's suppose you rode it out for about two weeks, but on March 23, 2020, you decided you had enough. You withdrew your money, and you stayed out for the rest of 2020. Not only did you lock in the losses of the bear market, but you also didn't get the advantage of any of the +66.8 percent gain that followed. This would be a textbook example of the Big Blunder as initial losses were exacerbated by the opportunity cost. Just because it was not actual dollars in the portfolio, doesn't eliminate the significance of the benefits that would have accrued to your account had it not been for the lost opportunity. The gains were there for the taking if only you had persevered and kept your emotions in check.

Figure 7.6

Employer's name, address, and ZIP code	Payer's RTN (optional)	OMB No. 1234-5678	Copy B
The Market		**2020**	For Recipient
		Form **1099 - FEAR**	This important hypothetical information illustrates the amount of gain this taxpayer lost due to panic during the COVID-19 crisis.
Control number	1 Interest income not included in box 3 $ income		
Employee's first name and initial Last name Suff.	2 Early withdrawal Penalty	3 Starting portfolio value on 3/11/20	
Chicken Little	$	$ 1,000,000.00	
123 Doomsday Blvd. Anytown, USA 12345	4 Federal income tax withheld	5 Fear tax as of 12/31/20 if not invested	
Employee's address and ZIP code	$	$ 361,421.00	
Form **1099 - FEAR**	(This is *NOT* an official tax form)		

> The fact is, if you had a $1 million investment account and were to receive a 1099 for the actual loss plus the opportunity cost of being absent during the run up in the market, your fear tax in 2020 would have amounted to $361,421.
>
> When making investment decisions, you must consider opportunity costs to understand the full advantage, or disadvantage, of any choices you make. We all tend to feel that we pay enough in taxes already. If you can understand how markets work, the fear tax is one tax you should never be forced to pay.

SECRET TO MANAGING EMOTIONS: Understanding *Long-Term*

We said it before but cannot emphasize the danger enough: the financial media clings to the charade that consistently timing the market is not only possible, but expected. Your fear is their fuel to drive this false narrative. To counter this, you must know unequivocally that managing your market emotions depends on your thorough understanding of the concept of *long-term* investing.

The first law of investment wisdom is this:
Long-term returns are the only ones that really matter.

The second law is:
All portfolios are long-term in nature. (With a few exceptions.)

Those exceptions would include portfolios designed to save for a down payment on a house, saving to pay off a short-term business note, or for putting money aside for a college education. In all these cases, the money has a defined end date when it will all be used for a specific expenditure. Even at that, the college education fund should be invested for capital appreciation, especially early in a child's life.

If a nest egg is needed for any type of income generation, it should be considered a long-term investment. With modern medicine today, it's entirely possible that a retiree will spend as much time in their retirement years as they did in their working years. The temptation for many nearing retirement is to go to a large bond or fixed-income position to "protect" the investment and get yield. Yet, as we have seen, the total return for stocks versus bonds is not even close, especially when inflation and taxes are considered. Even money that is set aside for an inheritance should be positioned to grow and benefit the heirs or institutions for whom it is intended.

We often say that investing should be dull. It shouldn't be exciting. More like watching paint dry or grass grow. If you want excitement, take a one-hundred-dollar bill and put it on a horse with a funny name. You will be thrilled for 90 to 120 seconds (and one *Benjamin* poorer).

Furthermore, by buying and holding thousands of companies in an EBI portfolio, you greatly increase the chances that you will own the winning companies. Someone might ask, "But don't we own a lot of losers as well?" It's true, you will own some companies that under perform for periods of time. In the worst case scenario, their value can even completely vanish, in which case you lose 100 percent of your purchase price. But the winners can potentially make 100 percent, 1,000 percent, or 10,000 percent. Miss just one or two of these winning stocks, and your entire portfolio will be affected.

Warren Buffett is an anomaly in the investing world as exhibited by his notoriety. (How many other superstar investors can you name?) He is also not an active manager you could hire. He's owned five hundred to six hundred stocks during his lifetime and made most of his money on about a dozen of them. At age ninety-two, he's also made 95 percent of his fortune after he turned sixty-five.[10] He is a living testament to long-term thinking.

Figure 7.7

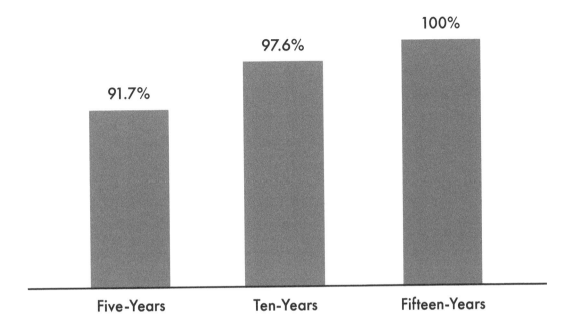

As seen in Figure 7.7, when any calendar five-year rolling time period for the S&P 500 Index® is examined, positive returns occurred nearly 92 percent of the time during this eighty-four-year timeframe. When ten-year or fifteen-year rolling time periods are observed, positive returns occur 97 to 100 percent of the time. Furthermore, since 1929 to 1932, the S&P 500 Index® has never had a four-year period when it lost ground each year.

The most recent three-year losing streak was from 2000 through 2002. However, just like clockwork, in 2003 the market came back, growing a healthy +28.7 percent, followed by five more positive years from 2004 through 2008 and then another twelve out of thirteen positive years through 2021.

Maybe We Should Pray for a Bad Year

Naturally, we are not seriously suggesting you bow your head and ask for difficult times. But certainly Evidence-Based Investment portfolio investors should have far less anxiety in bad years if they remain disciplined and steadfast in their strategy.

By taking a close look at results of the EBI 100 percent equity model over a thirty-two-year period, we see that each time a "bad year(s)" occurred, the results in the following years were phenomenal (Figure 7.8).[11]

Figure 7.8

Year	MRP Equity	Year	MRP Equity
1990	−16.4%	2006	21.5%
1991	23.2%	2007	7.6%
1992	−0.2%	2008	−39.8%
1993	21.7%	2009	39.9%
1994	5.9%	2010	19.4%
1995	20.7%	2011	−5.5%
1996	16.2%	2012	17.0%
1997	16.2%	2013	28.3%
1998	14.1%	2014	5.4%
1999	20.9%	2015	−3.0%
2000	−1.7%	2016	14.6%
2001	−5.2%	2017	23.2%
2002	−13.5%	2018	−9.8%
2003	40.8%	2019	26.8%
2004	19.6%	2020	14.3%
2005	12.1%	2021	22.6%

> In the seven post-bad-market periods after 1990, 1992, 1999, 2000–02, 2008, 2011, 2015, and 2018, the average annual return was +19.7 percent. A $100,000 portfolio invested in a tax-deferred retirement account on January 2, 1990, would have grown to $1,934,693 by December 31, 2021.
>
> These historical data give us confidence that a superdiversified EBI portfolio strategy buffers the ill effects of bad years and allows us to prosper in the inevitable and more frequent good-market periods.
>
> We just need to maintain a long-term perspective.

SUMMARY: Managing Your Emotions

Combining an implacable faith in long-term financial markets with super-diversification and portfolio optimization takes away the need or stress that comes with trying to predict the future. Understanding these fundamentals will enable you to keep your investment head clear even when those around you are losing theirs.

Because of the dulcet tones of Wall Street sirens and their ever-funded marketing machine, you must either "stop your ears" or "tie yourself to the mast" to avoid the Big Blunder of panicking out of the market. It's the worst of all unforced errors, which occurs when investors are guided by headlines instead of history when they think in terms of days instead of decades. You now have absolutely no excuse to *ever* make that mistake.

Key Points

- **Managing unwarranted fear is Job 1 of successful investing.** While wars, pandemics, or elections can create short-term market downturns, none of these are long-term actionable.

- **The Fear Tax is the biggest tax you can ever pay.** It is easily avoided by investors who understand markets and stay the course no matter the external market conditions.
- **Every portfolio is long-term and should be managed accordingly.** Short-term savings goals for a home down payment or emergency funds are liquid in nature, and thus not investment portfolios.
- **Should we pray for a bad year in the markets?** Not literally. But the evidence shows that periods following significant market downturns tend to rebound in a robust and rapid fashion.

Up next: as with almost anything in life, it's about *follow-through*.

CHAPTER 8

Hire the Right Coach

"The two most powerful warriors are patience and time."[1]

—Leo Tolstoy, *War and Peace*, 1867

If we were to ask, "Who is the greatest golfer of the last twenty-five years?", even someone with no interest in the game whatsoever could likely answer it correctly. But you know what?

Even Tiger Woods needs a coach.

Tiger doesn't need anyone to tell him how to play golf. He clearly knows how to win with fifteen major championship trophies in his man cave. The coolness and equanimity with which he conducts himself on the course as millions watch on TV—whether after a great shot or a poor one—is extraordinary. Nobody asks if Tiger is intelligent enough to be a great golfer. He attended Stanford and is clearly an exceptionally bright person. But it's not all about IQ in golf. Tiger's *temperament* and *coachability* is his secret. It's the same in investing.

Like each of us, Tiger needs someone who can take his goals, understand what his (few) limitations are, and help to guide him. He knows that great coaches make a measurable difference. They all start with the fundamentals, but they know the most important aspect of success in any endeavor lies within the space between the ears of their players. Naming goals, visualizing success, and connecting that success to their deepest values can lead to extraordinary results.

We ourselves have personal financial advisors even though we are writing a book about investing. Furthermore, the manuscript for this book was reviewed by a select group of more than two-dozen readers, which included clients, colleagues, friends, and family of all ages, and diverse backgrounds and perspectives. Their input and outtakes were critical to this project.

Let's face it. We all have a few things we need help with in our "game." How about you? Are your financial needs, wants, and wishes the same as they were ten years ago? Have you had a setback or a windfall that affects your thinking? Do you know what your strengths and weaknesses are when it comes to managing your financial life? Do you have a plan on how to get better?

If Tiger wanted to become a better golfer, he could do so, to a large extent, on his own. But stop and think. Is there any sport that you do not see a coach on the sidelines? Regardless of past success or current challenges, players of all sports, from all countries and all time periods, understand the importance of discipline to rise to the top. They also understand this in common: discipline is only possible with accompanying accountability and wise advice. That's why successful people in every serious endeavor—without exception—have a coach.

You're no different. Don't make excuses. You need to take action and find an advisor or coach who can help make a difference for you.

BLIND SPOTS: Eliminating the Big Three

As we have discussed, our biases can create blind spots in our understanding of what it is we should do. We've already seen several biases that affect investing decisions. Here are three more that can negatively affect investors, particularly if they don't have an advisor that can help them make sense of a complicated subject.

1. **Recency bias.** This plays out when we want to naturally incorporate more recent events into our decision-making process. But all of us know from experience that past events may be more important in understanding the wisdom needed for a big decision. Advisors with many years under their belt (we recommend at least ten years of experience) have wisdom that comes from having seen the issues you are facing now hundreds, if not thousands, of times before. This bed of knowledge and experience is something a coach in any field has that all outside of their field cannot possibly acquire.
2. **Status-quo bias.** Chances are you've had the same television satellite or cable provider for some time even though there are new expanded-streaming options now available. Why? Because like most, you aren't excited about change. It's easier to simply stay where you are and not worry about it. The right coach can motivate you to make changes that are highly advantageous—in matters much more consequential than your television programming—like the nest egg that will fund your retirement years.
3. **Sunk-cost bias.** Sometimes called the "sunk-cost fallacy," this is a cousin to the status-quo bias because it is about hanging on to something (product or decision) that should be let go. Bad investment decisions fall right in the middle of this bias. The right advisor will identify these instances and help investors correct them without the emotional attachment.

A qualified coach or advisor will reduce the negative impact of biases by simply enabling clients to act in their own best interests by giving them a clear line of sight.

First Things First: Do Some Research

You deserve to have the finest financial coach available. It's your financial well-being at stake, and choice of an advisor is a very serious decision that you must get right the first time. When undertaking the search for the right fit for you, we suggest you start with areas you can usually research online.

We consider these three areas must-haves:

1. **Are they independent?** The definition we're looking for in this context is: having no association with any entities that adversely affect objectivity. This list of entities could include banks, insurance companies, traditional wire (stockbroker) houses, and broker-dealers (even ones that say they are "independent"). This particularly applies to advisors connected with *public* financial companies, which have a duty to stockholders first and individual investment clients second.

    A truly independent firm is organized simply as a Registered Investment Advisor (RIA) compensated with fees collected *directly* from the client. This direct-pay arrangement gives the independent firm the ability to seek the best solutions for the client while minimizing the chance of a misaligned interest. This eliminates incentives to push certain products that are often associated with parent-company arrangements. The bottom line is that an independent Registered Investment Advisor acts in a *fiduciary* manner that seeks to eliminate any conflicts of interest and applies the highest professional standard while having an obligation to consider the client's best interests first.

2. **What is their experience and professional qualifications?** *Knowledge × Experience = Wisdom*. And who would deny that if there is one thing we need today, it's more *wisdom* in all areas. Unfortunately, the financial services industry is known for being an aggressive recruiter of inexperienced sales representatives. In fact, 80 to 90 percent of financial advisors fail in the first three years.[2] The Certified Financial Planner® (CFP®) practitioner is the benchmark for the industry. We would not recommend any firm that did not have this same standard among its advisors.

3. **Do they use a team approach?** A common misperception is that larger financial firms are better equipped by mere virtue of their size.

However, in most cases, large national firms are government-like bureaucracies that just lease space to individual representatives in their offices.

In our view, boutique independent firms are typically better at building a team that can collectively devote their knowledge and energies to a client's best interests. We call this fiduciary organizational intelligence. Working as a true team means that all clients are clients of the firm—not clients of individual advisors within the firm. This helps with continuity in the event something happens to specific advisors and they are no longer part of the firm for any reason. Additionally, in independent firms, the owners or principals are more likely to be directly accessible to clients.

If these first three areas cannot be sufficiently vetted on a firm's website, then a phone interview is also a good way to filter advisor candidates. Once again, if an advisory firm cannot pass these initial must-have standards, we would suggest saving yourself time and frustration by moving on to find one who can.

HIRING AN ADVISOR: Questions to Ask

Socrates famously said, "My way toward the truth is to ask the right questions."[3] Once you find a firm or two who have cleared the must-have hurdles, you'll want to visit their physical location. Below are three questions that will provide a good assessment to determine a right fit. We recommend that you ask them exactly as scripted and in the order they appear.

Let's start with an important question (an easy one for you):

1. **What is your investment philosophy, and how will you manage my portfolio?** Obviously, any investment advice that involves active management techniques (timing or picking), should be summarily dismissed. Remember, capitalism creates wealth, advisors don't. The advisor's job is

to help you harness the broad market returns you're entitled to and thus protect your all-important purchasing power. So, listen carefully for the words "evidence-based investing" in their answer. Only trust an advisor who trusts the market.

2. **Where will my investments be held?** While this may be a "no-brainer," a legitimate advisor will only use third-party *custodians* to hold your funds. (Fidelity and Schwab are well-known examples.) These institutions will provide monthly reporting of your account statements and be available for any questions in addition to providing secure online access to your accounts. You should never be in a position where the advisor reports account holdings directly. (Bernie Madoff is the classic bad actor. He "generated" fake statements for all his clients from his own computer.)

3. **Do you invest in the same investments as your clients?** When we're asked this question, we often simply pull up one of our personal accounts on the screen so we can show that we're in exactly the same types of investments we would put our clients in. Don't be afraid to ask the same of your prospective advisor. There's no better way to check their commitment to their philosophy and process than to see if they "put their money where their mouth is."

How a Coach Should Help

With technical expertise as a given, the obvious advantage of having a financial coach is to be there to remind us how to handle the psychological temptations we all face as investors. They also help provide motivation and emotional support when needed. Lack of awareness and lack of confidence are always obstacles to meaningful change. Coaches help us remove both.

As we enter the home stretch of discussion on creating a worry-free lifelong-investment experience, we offer three important disciplines, which should be maintained with the expert help of your new coach.

DISCIPLINE #1: Create an Investment Policy Statement (IPS)

Lewis Carroll once said, "If you don't know where you're going, any road will get you there."[4] As the author of the famous *Alice's Adventures in Wonderland*, his quote is germane for our discussion as you must strive to avoid any "wormholes" that might get you off course. For your investment portfolio, your roadmap is the Investment Policy Statement.

First, think of your IPS as essentially a sort of high-level business plan for your portfolio. As such, it defines the roles and responsibilities of the advisory relationship and also becomes a collaborative document so that you, as an investor, can take responsibility for communicating any life changes or changes in financial circumstances that might affect the management of your portfolio. It should include a summary of your comprehensive financial picture as well as your primary financial goals, wishes, and wants for the funds being invested.

Second, with the overall primary financial goals established, portfolio risk levels which are appropriate for your circumstances can be assessed. The three key areas of risk are:

1. **Need** to take risk. After Secured Income Sources (i.e., Social Security, pensions, royalties, etc.) are totaled, it can be determined what additional cash flow needs to be generated by an investment portfolio. This guides an advisor to help ensure that your dollars don't run out before your days do. It is of particular importance for retirees. (As advisors, we've heard over and over that the greatest fear of any parent is becoming a burden to their kids because they did not plan their finances properly.)

2. **Ability** to take risk. This is a practical metric that depends on the investment time horizon and the size of the portfolio. A young professional has decades of earnings potential remaining, while a retiree may have little or no real earned-income (salary) opportunities left.

3. **Willingness** to take risk. This area of risk is what most people refer to as personal "risk tolerance." It deals with an individual's level of

comfort and how they might respond to potential loss in their portfolio. While it's an important factor to explore for an investor, this is the most emotional of the three areas of risk. As such, it is unwise to allow this area to fully dictate portfolio allocation decisions.

By considering all three areas of a risk profile, you can put yourself in a favorable footing to optimize your portfolio.

Third, the IPS can now be used to outline investment goals and objectives, and describe the strategies that the advisor will employ to meet them. Besides risk tolerance, specific information on matters such as asset allocation between stocks and bonds, tax considerations, drift limitations, liquidity requirements, and unique circumstances should be included. If done correctly, the IPS enables you to stay focused on the long-term goals. This is a critical safeguard against potential emotional mistakes (like running aground on the rocks near the Sirens).

Finally, the IPS should establish the frequency of monitoring and procedures for making any future changes to the IPS. It should also specify the reasons *not* to change any policies based on short-term market performance. The IPS can also have "key terms" and "disclosures" for quick reference.

The next discipline involves a critical, but often overlooked, strategy of maintaining target portfolio allocations within stock-bond drift limits outlined in your Investment Policy Statement.

DISCIPLINE #2: Implement Periodic Rebalancing

We already know from our discussion of "when to get in the market" at the end of Chapter 1 that, overall, we always want to be fully invested. Left to our judgement affected by emotions, we are more likely to either hold losing investments too long hoping they come back, or keep winners hoping they are not finished growing.

That's why it's imperative to create and maintain a process designed to systematically sell a portion of the asset classes that have risen in value, and subsequently to buy more of the asset classes that might be lagging behind—either not growing as fast or perhaps losing value in certain time periods.

How Periodic Rebalancing Actually Works

First, we assume that you have hired a great advisor or coach who determines just the right stock-bond allocation based on your risk tolerance and personal needs, wants, and wishes—which are documented in your personal Investment Policy Statement.

Next, let's assume you have a 60 to 40 portfolio mix of stocks to bonds (Figure 8.1). This mix will naturally change over time as market fluctuations occur. Let's say a year later, the mix is 65 to 35 because stocks have outpaced bonds. Conversely, it may be 55 to 45 if stocks have retreated during the period. At any rate, the rebalancing will involve your advisor resetting the mix to the original 60 to 40 allocation.

To accomplish this, the growing asset class is sold down to its original allocation. That cash is then reallocated into the asset class that shrunk to rebalance the portfolio (Figure 8.2). We would reiterate that this is not a market timing attempt, but simply allow the market to tell us when to buy and sell to reset a portfolio to it's prescribed risk tolerance level. This market-driven auto-rebalancing creates a fail-safe for optimizing your portfolio allocation.

Figure 8.1

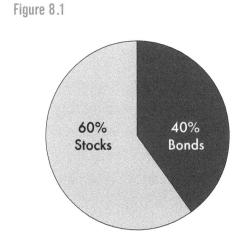

Figure 8.2

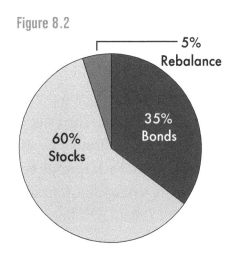

One common question we get from investors of retirement age is, "How do we get income from our nest egg once we've retired?" They don't want to be forced to sell investments for household cashflow when their value is down. This is why rebalancing becomes particularly important with managing your portfolio once you've entered your retirement years. So, how is this cash flow accomplished?

First of all, retirees should be taking money for living expenses from the cash or fixed income side of their portfolios. As we mentioned in Chapter 6, retirees should also hold shorter-term, high-quality bonds, which have far less volatility. Naturally, when money is taken from the cash/bond side of the portfolio, it reduces the percentage remaining in that asset class.

In the same way we just mentioned (Figures 8.1 and 8.2), when the rebalancing takes place—in this case because of a withdrawal instead of market fluctuations—equities are sold to replenish the cash/bonds position. Consequently, a retiree is only selling the stock asset classes that are higher to replenish the cash/bond side. If for some reason all stock asset classes are in an extreme bear market, which you now know is rare, then it may require holding off on the rebalancing for a limited period of time.

However, even in the deepest of recessions or bear markets, there are typically one or two stock asset classes that are not down, or perhaps are just flat. Knowing what we know about stock-market cycles, if retirees have at least *four* years of living expenses in the cash/bond allocation, there is a reasonable chance that they can weather any market storm and have adequate cash flow through a down market without having to sell equities when they are low. Most retirees have room to allocate even five or more years of living expenses if they want extra-restful sleep. The crux of this strategy is having a *margin of safety* that allows you the endurance to stick around long enough to let the resilience of the market move back in your favor after any downturn.

Another important question we get often is, "How can we best handle the huge threat of inflation?" Remember the paradigm-shifting truth that real, long-term, *purchasing-power* protection comes through owning stocks. Given this, it's simply a matter of maintaining asset-class-allocation integrity through periodic rebalancing as companies work to manage the challenge that inflation brings with it. However, even if the companies you own in your portfolio are doing their job, you and your coach still need to handle the rebalancing process correctly to avoid a major unforced error.

Figure 8.3 shows just how important periodic rebalancing is over the course of a thirty-year retirement.[5] Notice we are looking at a period of time when inflation was very high. Between 1974–83, it averaged over 8 percent. The graph shows a moderate allocation of 60 percent stocks, 30 percent bonds, and 10 percent treasury bills (essentially cash).

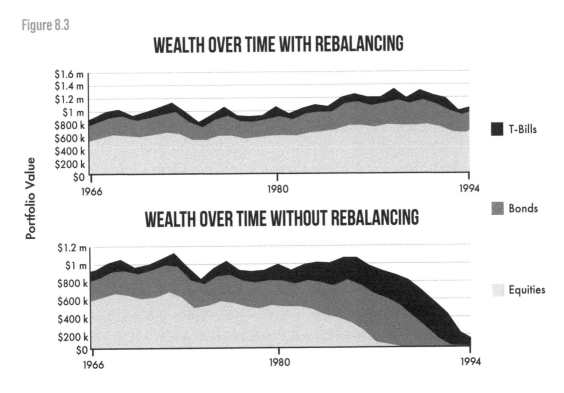

Figure 8.3

Both portfolios assume a 4 percent withdrawal rate with an annual withdrawal adjustment for inflation. The rates of return are assumed to be the same in both. The difference was simply that the top portfolio was rebalanced. The bottom one was not.

The lesson is a simple one: don't underestimate the incredible impact rebalancing has in your portfolio. Herein, the rebalancing discipline illustrates yet one more advantage of an EBI approach to investing and the peace of mind it will bring you.

DISCIPLINE #3: Manage for Tax Efficiency

Every CPA has the same line they use on April 15, right before they give us the unwelcome news of how much we owe: "The only thing worse than having to pay taxes is not having to pay them." This usually provides little solace, but we get it. The ability to earn a living in the greatest nation on earth is a privilege and a blessing. This brings us to our third discipline of *managing for tax efficiency*.

Tax-Loss Harvesting

For portfolio tax efficiency, we use a technique called *tax-loss harvesting*. It's a relatively straightforward concept that is used surprisingly little. Simply put, you sell some investments at a loss to offset gains you've realized by selling other stocks at a profit. The result is that you only pay taxes on your net profit, or the amount you've gained minus the amount you lost, thereby reducing your tax bill. Tax-loss harvesting offers the biggest benefit when you use it to reduce regular income, since tax rates on income typically run higher than rates on long-term capital gains.

The tax-loss harvesting strategy often requires a consideration between taxable and non-taxable accounts, so we recommend also engaging your CPA since they typically have a broader perspective concerning your overall personal tax situation.

Reduce Turnover

When making changes in taxable accounts, it should be done carefully because minimizing the impact of taxes on returns is an important aspect of optimizing your portfolio. Practically speaking, this means rebalancing only when significant drift has occurred. We typically recommend using a 5/25 rule. That is, rebalancing when an asset class has drifted either an absolute 5 percent from its target or a relative 25 percent.

For example, if an asset class has a target of 30 percent of your total portfolio, rebalancing should occur when the allocation falls below 25 percent or rises above 35 percent (the absolute 5 percent rule is the determining factor). If an asset class has a target of 10 percent, the rebalancing would be triggered at either 7.5 percent or 12.5 percent (the relative 25 percent rule is the determining factor). By allowing a bit of drift to occur, you can minimize the impact of taxes without losing control over the risk level of your portfolio.

Furthermore, if you maintain both taxable and tax-qualified retirement accounts (IRAs, 401K, etc.) you may often have the opportunity to focus on rebalancing in the tax-qualified accounts first. This combination of rebalancing with tax-loss harvesting could help minimize tax consequences substantially. Remember, it's the *overall after-tax* return on your portfolio we are concerned with.

Avoid Short-Term Gains

Don't make the unforced error of taking short-term gains. This keeps you from being taxed at the higher (marginal) tax rates. Simply wait until the long-term holding period of one year is achieved. With all of this said, always seek the help of a tax professional who knows your specific tax situation.

SUMMARY: Maintaining Discipline

It's worth closing this discussion on discipline by reiterating that we believe *risk* in the investing context is simply a word that connotes a level of opportunity. We've shown you the history and behavior of markets from several vantage points in an effort to bolster your confidence in your long-term success. This in turn was designed to encourage you to take the proper amount of risk needed for you to meet your personal financial needs, wants, and wishes.

Our hope is that you now have a clearer understanding of why long-term investing should never be a scary prospect, but rather one that will allow you the opportunity to benefit from the free capital markets that you are blessed to be a part of. It's why we tell our clients that our favorite investment holding period is *forever*.

Finding the right professional help will protect you from the pessimism that Wall Street and the financial media continually cast your way. This doesn't mean there won't be market setbacks. As you now know, those are a normal part of the process. The right advisor will make sure a setback doesn't derail your plan. So now, with the right investing strategy and the right coach, you have the resolve to maintain discipline with your money from now on.

Key Points

- **Even Tiger Woods needs a coach.** He knows that, like all of us, he has blind spots that good advisors can see clearer.
- **Find the right coach for you.** This takes some research which includes the exact right questions to ask as an investor.
- **There are three areas of disciplines an advisor or coach should help you employ.** These provide the third-party, birds-eye view to increase the chances of a successful long-term investing experience.

You're now ready for the most important aspect of your investing plan.

CHAPTER 9

Focus on What Really Matters

> "To live in the hearts of those we leave behind is to never die."[1]
> —Jay Kristoff

wealth

[welth] *noun*

----

the value of one's time, talents, treasures, and relationships; abundance

Often, we ask clients to complete the following statement:

"True wealth is _____."

We get a variety of answers, but what's interesting is that the answers we receive are most often about things in life that are not defined by dollars and cents. That's because "true wealth" is what's left over when all the money is gone. In our conference room, we have a framed definition of the word *wealth*. We placed it there as a daily reminder to focus on the things that really matter: your time, your talents, and your relationships.

The definition of course includes money, within our *treasures*. The first eight chapters of this book were devoted to the financial aspect of your treasures to provide you with a worry-free investing framework. This was the first order of business that now enables you to focus on the more important aspects of your wealth.

Have you ever considered what makes something valuable? There are several things that can affect the value of an object. Perhaps it has a *usable* value, which pertains to its practicality of utility. It has a functional purpose that becomes necessary for everyday life. Or maybe it has some *aesthetic* value, which speaks of its beauty—whether extrinsic or intrinsic. Think of a beautiful piece of art, like the one hanging in our office foyer. While usefulness and beauty add significant value, nothing increases the value of something more than its scarcity. When there is a limited supply of a resource that is in high demand, people are willing to give almost anything to obtain more of it. Is this not true about the *time* we have been given on this earth? Our time is one of the scarcest, and thus most valuable, resources we possess. All are numbered. Therefore, we must consider each day as a gift of incredible value to steward wisely.

Perhaps you're like the many clients we serve who have spent the last three or four decades of their lives building successful careers and raising families. But now, as you consider your retirement years, you're faced with the question of how to spend potentially another thirty-plus years. How will you use the blessing of your remaining time? A *true wealth* advisor helps you address this important aspect of your total wealth.

What about your talents? These are the valuable gifts and abilities unique to you, and they should also not be wasted. Perhaps you developed skills throughout your career that can now be put to even greater use. Maybe it's time to start a business or ministry that impacts the lives of those around you. Regardless of who you are, there are valuable talents in your possession that will be lost once you're gone. How can you invest those talents now?

This brings us to the final and most important aspect of true wealth: our *relationships*. What if you could invest your time, talents, and treasures in a way that makes a decisive influence in the relationships you value the most?

Earning and having the opportunity to steward financial wealth is a worthy endeavor. Passing it along to those we love after our days are done is a natural and good thing. And while you might be tempted to leave your kids, and maybe even their kids, enough to do anything, we would most likely agree it's not wise to leave them so much that they can do *nothing*.

We believe it's not just about passing down what material wealth *we have*, it's also the wisdom that makes us who *we are* that will make the most impact on the next generation. We believe that the most important work we do as *true wealth* advisors is to help place our clients in a position to leave a complete and robust legacy for their children and grandchildren in all aspects.

We call this your *Return on Legacy*®.

We live in a time of unprecedented economic and social challenges. There are serious issues that are on the minds of all Americans who care about their family and the generations that will follow them. Handling the emotional and practical aspects associated with leaving not just financial capital but also life wisdom and spiritual capital will determine the ultimate success of your legacy.

EXAMPLE: High *Return on Legacy*®

Consider a man who lived three centuries ago. He, along with his dedicated wife, understood the importance of a high *Return on Legacy*®.

Jonathan Edwards was a Puritan minister in the 1700s. He was one of the most respected preachers in his day. He attended Yale at the age of thirteen and later went on to become the president of Princeton College. He married his wife, Sarah, in 1727, and they were blessed with eleven children. Every night when Mr. Edwards was home, he would spend an hour conversing with his family and then praying a blessing over each child. Jonathan and Sarah passed on a great legacy to their children.

An American educator, A.E. Winship, decided to trace the descendants of the Edwards almost 150 years after his death. His findings are remarkable. The Edwards's legacy includes:

- One US vice president
- One dean of a law school
- One dean of a medical school
- Three US senators

- Three governors
- Three mayors
- Thirteen college presidents
- Thirty judges
- Sixty doctors
- Sixty-five professors
- Seventy-five military officers
- Eighty public-office holders
- One hundred lawyers
- One hundred clergymen
- 285 college graduates.

Winship explains this extraordinary success, "Edwards was a God-fearing man; hard working, intelligent, and moral." Furthermore, Winship states, "Much of the capacity and talent, intensity, and character of the Edwards's family through the generations is due to Mrs. Edwards."[2]

The Edwards legacy provides an example of what some call the four-generation rule. How a parent raises their child—the love they give, the values they teach, the emotional environment they offer, the education they provide—influences not only their children but the four generations to follow, either for good or evil. What a challenging thought.

Every generation is strategic. We aren't responsible for the last generation. And we can't bear the full responsibility for the next generation. But we do have our generation. Like Jonathan and Sarah Edwards, we can decide how we fulfill our responsibilities in this age.

The Fourth Quarter

Sadly, Mr. Edwards died at the age of fifty-four—a short life by our modern medical standards. A study conducted on the US population found that the most productive age in life is between sixty to seventy years of age.

- The average age of Nobel Prize winners is sixty-two.
- The average age of the CEOs of prominent companies in the world is sixty-three.
- Nick Saban, considered the greatest college-football coach of all time by most, won five of his seven national championships in his sixties.

The second most productive stage of life is seventy to eighty, and interestingly, the average age of the pastors of the one hundred largest churches in the US is seventy-one.

Given these observations, we could make a strong case that the best years of our lives are between ages sixty and eighty. Otherwise known as the *Fourth Quarter*.

And what do you see every team do at the beginning of the fourth quarter without fail? They hold up four fingers. With that simple gesture they are saying to their teammates and supporters, "No matter what we did in the first three quarters, we know *it all comes down to this. We are pledging to finish as strong as we possibly can.*"

What about you?

It's Your Race to Run

The 4 x 400 relay is one of the most anticipated and exciting events in the Olympic games. And do you know what the most important key to winning that race is? Running the fastest? That certainly is one key. But far more important is the *handoff*. If either runner in the exchange drops the baton, the entire team loses the race. We would also note that each handoff is made when the passer is running near full speed.

Consider your handoff to the next leg of the relay. You have the opportunity to teach your children and grandchildren all of the wisdom you have acquired. Now assume that one day your grandchildren will teach their grandchildren in the same way. If that great-great grandchild of yours for some reason fails to pass on to their children the wisdom that started with you, then your instruction will *still* affect the lives of your loved ones for the next 150 years. Imagine what our world will look like a century and a half from now. The need for discernment and wisdom will be greater than ever. We truly believe that this generation has the potential to be exceptional. But let's face it, they need your help *right now* to make that happen!

So while we trust your confidence level about optimizing the return on your investments (ROI) has risen considerably as a result of this book, one day your financial wealth will end—one way or another. Having a plan for stewarding your legacy is just as important as having one for stewarding your investment portfolio. We would welcome the opportunity to help with yours. Regardless of whether or not Providence allows this, our hope is that the remainder of your days can also be filled with optimizing your *Return on Legacy*® (ROL), the only "return" that doesn't have to end.

> ### An Invaluable Gift of Legacy
>
> One of the greatest gifts that can be left for loved ones is your story and your wisdom *in writing*. It's an effective way for parents to share the memories and joys of their life while also creating a cherished legacy for you and the entire family. One book that helps you do this is *Dad, I Want to Hear Your Story*.[3] It's designed to guide a father—and mother—with over 250 prompts and questions, making it fun and easy to share the stories of their childhood, teens, and adult years. This will be the tales of life's victories, challenges, and lessons.
>
> I (Jim) have experienced the power of this in my own life. When I lost my first wife to cancer, it left our two boys, ages ten and fourteen, without a mom at critical ages. Having been made aware of this "father questions" concept, I decided to go through the exercise and present a bound gift for our boys upon their high school graduation. It made a considerable and lasting impact for them.
>
> For grandparents, *Tell Me Your Life Story, Grandpa (or Grandma)* is equally designed to elicit treasured memories.[4] It asks over two hundred questions that creates an invaluable keepsake that can be passed down for generations to come.
>
> This is a great place to start to create a legacy like none other.

Afterword

"There are risks to action; but they are far less than the long-term risks of comfortable inaction."[1]
—John F. Kennedy

We had a choice to make concerning our own *Return on Legacy*®.

Remain comfortable or take a risk.

I (Jim) was blessed to have scaled the mountain in our profession and sell my wealth management firm in Dallas in my early fifties. This enabled me for a season to become a full-time author, speaker, and adjunct professor at my beloved alma mater. I was living my dream. By his thirtieth birthday, Matt was also a successful CEO of his own independent wealth-management firm. His success afforded him the flexibility to devote a portion of his schedule to the ministry of his church community. There was no apparent reason we might come together as business partners, or as coauthors, other than that the more we talked, the more we saw a need that required action.

When need, ability, and passion come together, it creates a *mission*.

And so, our mission, if you will, is to reach as many as will listen to provide them with a worry-free investment framework you've now discovered:

- **Free markets are the economic "miracle" of all of history.**
    - ▷ The right time to invest in always *now*.
    - ▷ *Stay invested* to avoid the Big Blunder.

- **Avoid the fallacious methods of Wall Street and its minions.**
    - ▷ Timing and picking the market is a fool's errand.
    - ▷ Chasing returns will only disappoint in the long run.

- **EBI principles optimize an investment portfolio in the long run. Generally:**
    - ▷ Stocks hedge against inflation, and their returns exceed bond returns.
    - ▷ Small company returns exceed large companies.
    - ▷ "Value" company returns exceed "growth" companies.

- *Worry-free* **investing of treasure allows for leaving a legacy of** *true* **wealth.**
    - ▷ How you spend your time and talents.
    - ▷ Pouring wisdom into your most cherished relationships.

In the Introduction, we mentioned the three most common mistakes we've seen investors make over our combined half-century in the wealth-management business.

1. Taking unnecessary risk with poorly constructed portfolios.
2. Missing out on market returns (optimizers) that are available to all.
3. Losing money on poor decisions made due to weak or nonexistent professional advice.

And now, we would add one more:
4. Failing to leave a legacy beyond money.

AFTERWORD

We promised we would ask you the same question again. So here it is with a slight variation:

> **On a scale of 1 to 10, with "10" being "perfectly," how confident are you that you now have the tools and motivation to manage your *true wealth*?**

We anticipate that your score went up since the Introduction! Our hope is that you now feel equipped to never find yourself involved with any of these four mistakes again. To this end, we trust you consider our efforts to bring these issues to light have been worth the investment of time you've made with us.

Thank you for "examining the evidence."

May God bless you and keep you always.

Jim and Matt

Postscript: Faith-Driven Investing

"Honor the Lord with your wealth."[1]
—Proverbs 3:9

As you enter the reception area of our office, you will be greeted with a colorful painting that we named simply, "Evidence." We commissioned this work from a well-known artist from Miami, Salvador "Salvi" Lorenzo. His resume of artistic awards from around the world is lengthy, and Salvi's story of his razor's edge escape from Fidel Castro's Cuba could fill the silver screen, easily capturing your attention for two hours.

As we tried to describe what we were looking for him to create as the centerpiece of our office, Psalms 19:1 came to mind.

"The heavens declare the glory of God;
And the firmament shows his handiwork."[2]

Salvi understood immediately what we were looking for. He created a palate with bright colors depicting a man surveying his fields at dusk. We imagined the old and wise gentleman farmer, after another exhausting day of work, praising God for the little corner of the world He had made for a time, just for him.

Our goal was to have a work of art front and center in our workspace that would convey in at least a subtle way that . . .

God owns it all.

If you're a Christian, this statement is a familiar one. As the psalmist stated above, it's the first and fundamental truth of the created universe.

As advisors who strive to maintain a biblical worldview, we also understand and embrace the idea that none of what we have is really ours, but rather we are simply stewards of what we have been blessed to manage for a time. If you agree with this core belief, then adding an "eternal dimension" to your investing strategy can give you an option that aligns your faith *with* your finances.

There are over $40 trillion invested with financial advisors in the United States. Of that, it's estimated that about $4 trillion (10 percent) is stewarded by families of faith. Yet less than 1 percent of those dollars are intentionally invested in faith-driven investments.

Many are surprised to learn there are nearly 2,500 passages in the Bible dealing with money and economics in some form; that's over two thousand more times than either *faith* (346) or *love* (361) are mentioned. Jesus talked about financial matters more than any other topic with eleven of his thirty-nine parables dealing with money. Based on this evidence alone, it's obvious that God considers how we handle our finances to be of the utmost importance.

Just as with Adam's charge, our stewardship comes with serious responsibilities. In the New Testament, the Parable of the Talents (Matthew 25: 14–30)[3] provides a keen insight as to just how serious.

> "For it will be like a man going on a journey, who called his servants and entrusted to them his property. To one he gave five talents, to another two, to another one, to each according to his ability. Then he went away. He who had received the five talents went at once and traded with them, and he made five talents more. So also he who had the two talents made two talents more. But he who had received the one talent went and dug in the ground and hid his master's money. Now after a long time the

master of those servants came and settled accounts with them. And he who had received the five talents came forward, bringing five talents more, saying, 'Master, you delivered to me five talents; here, I have made five talents more.' His master said to him, 'Well done, good and faithful servant. You have been faithful over a little; I will set you over much. Enter into the joy of your master.' And he also who had the two talents came forward, saying, 'Master, you delivered to me two talents; here, I have made two talents more.' His master said to him, 'Well done, good and faithful servant. You have been faithful over a little; I will set you over much. Enter into the joy of your master.' He also who had received the one talent came forward, saying, 'Master, I knew you to be a hard man, reaping where you did not sow, and gathering where you scattered no seed, so I was afraid, and I went and hid your talent in the ground. Here, you have what is yours.' But his master answered him, 'You wicked and slothful servant! You knew that I reap where I have not sown and gather where I scattered no seed? Then you ought to have invested my money with the bankers, and at my coming I should have received what was my own with interest. So take the talent from him and give it to him who has the ten talents. For to everyone who has will more be given, and he will have an abundance. But from the one who has not, even what he has will be taken away. And cast the worthless servant into the outer darkness. In that place there will be weeping and gnashing of teeth.'"

Now a talent was a lot of money. The common talent in the first century consisted of approximately 130 pounds of gold. At press time, spot gold prices were in the $1,700–1,800-per-ounce range. In today's dollars, that would equate on the low end to about $3.5 million, $7 million, and $17.5 million for the one, two, and five talents, respectively.

We can understand from the passage that the Master expected a solid return for the investments he entrusted to these servants. It's notable that the Master was fair and just in that he did not require more from the servants than they were able to give. Two of the three were praised for their efforts and results, and even told, "Well done, good and faithful servants." A familiar phrase we all long to hear one day.

The third servant, with only one talent under his responsibility, seems to have had a good motive: keep the original sum safe no matter what. In fact, he reasoned to himself that by simply burying it, his master would be pleased with his "principal preservation" strategy given that he was a hard man. The servant was mistaken.

The Master was in no way pleased.

In fact, the Master called the servant "wicked" and "slothful." He said to "cast the wicked servant into outer darkness." It must have been a shock to hear those words. The application for this passage typically involves an encouragement to use our God-given talents (different definition) and financial resources for the advancement of God's Kingdom. But as financial advisors who are also striving to be faithful servants, we asked a deeper question.

What if we took our own money—and that of our clients who have hired us—and unwittingly invested it in the campaign of the Enemy "while our Master is away"?[4]

We are talking about owning the stocks of US companies who profit from things like gambling, pornography, abortion, human trafficking, etc. The list could go on. Or perhaps winnowing out all Chinese companies because many, if not most, use forced labor. Unfortunately, as cultural attitudes have moved away from biblical standards, there has been a significant increase in the number of companies whose bottom lines are benefitting from these activities both at home and abroad. If this is a troubling thought for you as it is for us, then you may want to seriously consider a Faith-Driven Investing strategy.

FAITH-DRIVEN INVESTING: How It Works

Technology over the last decade has allowed ways to set up screens for company stocks so that your portfolio can be largely free of companies that profit from products, services, or activities that contradict biblical values. We say "largely" because like anything in our fallen world, perfection is not possible. But advanced-screening tools can remove the vast majority of direct violations. In addition, private alternative options are now also available.

Another way to look at this is to simply ask the question, "What would my Master be displeased to have me invest His money in?" This is not out of a judgmental attitude, but rather it's because we love the Master because of His love for us. Doesn't it then follow that we should love what He loves? Are we not exhorted also to hate what He hates (Psalm 97:10)?[5]

Since you're already familiar with Evidence-Based Investing, you can see in Figure A.1 how we start with the EBI process and then apply additional screens to provide Faith-Driven Investment options.

Figure A.1

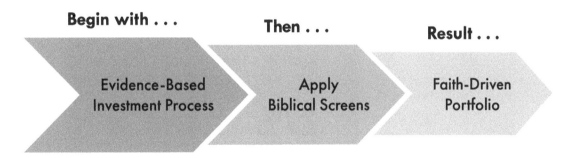

Practical Implementation

Step 1: Typically, a faith-driven investment advisor would ask you to take a brief survey which allows you to express your personal values to begin the process of aligning your faith with your finances. This usually consists of simply rating on a negative/positive scale up to fifty separate issues based on your values. Figure A.2 is a sample from the survey.

Figure A.2

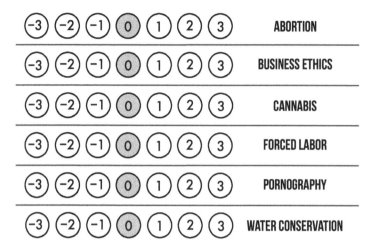

Step 2: Once your personal values are provided via the survey, it is overlayed to create an "X-ray" of your current portfolio statements to see how well your investments align with your values. Here is a SAMPLE page from the X-rayed portfolio report (Figure A.3).

Figure A.3

PORTFOLIO SCREENING REPORT
John and Mary Smith
Report as of October 10, 2023

27%
VALUES ALIGNMENT

MOST ALIGNED		LEAST ALIGNED	
Company Name	% Alined	Company Name	% Alined
McClure & Sons	87%	Fibonacci & Co.	6%
Kutch Group	65%	Dark Side Capital	7%
Reinger Group	44%	Gold Rush Inc.	11%
Batz Inc.	41%	Active Managers Co.	20%
Page LLC	40%	XYZ Co.	24%

POSTSCRIPT: FAITH-DRIVEN INVESTING

The report shows that only 27 percent of the companies contained in the investor's portfolio are aligned with the investor's values. However, assuming this was a $1 million portfolio, it could be said that $730,000 (73 percent) violates their personal values. This situation is not unusual.

Step 3: Create an alternative portfolio using an evidence-based framework, but also filter the holdings to align with the clients' values. It might look more like Figure A.4.

Figure A.4

PORTFOLIO SCREENING REPORT
John and Mary Smith
October 10, 2023

91%
VALUES ALIGNMENT

MOST ALIGNED

Company Name	% Alined
Evidence Wealth LLC	100%
Mertz-Langworth	100%
Quigley Group	100%
Jackie & Gleason	100%
Hansen PLC	99%

LEAST ALIGNED

Company Name	% Alined
Hermiston Ltd	85%
Gaylord PLC	89%
Powlowski and Toy	90%
Heaney & Goodwin	91%
Batz-Koch	92%

While a score of 100 percent is ideal, nothing in this life resides in the "perfect" category, including a faith-driven-portfolio allocation. But, as you can see, we can get very close at 91 percent. The fact that in a $1 million portfolio, this reallocation to a faith-driven-portfolio structure would have taken back almost $650,000 from the campaign of the Enemy is a win for God's Kingdom by any account.

What About Faith-Driven Investing Returns?

This is a common question when investors first learn about Faith-Driven Investing: "Will my portfolio returns suffer as a result of screening out some highly profitable companies?" To answer this question, let's look at an independent study (Figure A.5).

Figure A.5

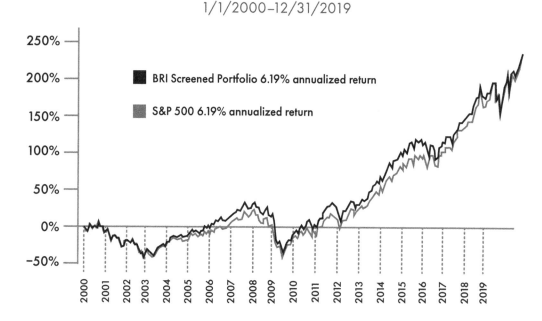

The Biblically Responsible Investing Institute (BRII) took on the task of assessing the effect of screening the S&P 500 Index® over a recent twenty-year period ending in 2019. The results support the idea that investors of faith who desire to align their investments with biblical principles can do so without compromising return. Figure A.5 tracks a portfolio of companies passing BRII's comprehensive biblical screens versus the unscreened index. As can be seen, in the long-term there is no negative effect from Faith-Driven Investing. The BRII screening experienced a slim disadvantage in some periods and a small advantage in others. But overall, the analysis showed an identical return over the two-decade period. [6]

What can we learn from this study?

Opposite of what some may assume, investors seeking to incorporate their faith into their investments don't have to surrender returns to do so. Now there is no way to guarantee that this kind of success will persist in the future. However, we can reasonably take some reassurance from the results of this analysis.

Build Your Own Fund

As your account values grow over your lifetime, you may have the opportunity to move into another level of Faith-Driven Investing: building your own fund.

The generic term for this is a *separately managed account*, or SMA. In SMAs, unlike in mutual funds, you *directly* own the securities held in individual accounts. This direct ownership allows customized screens that help you choose and include exactly the individual companies that align with your values and preferences. Again, the question to ask is, "What would my Master be pleased to have me invest His money in?"

In an SMA, tax management becomes much easier and more efficient through the afore mentioned tax-loss harvesting technique (Chapter 8). Once you have determined your investment strategy per your Investment Policy Statement, your advisor should do a Tax Transition Analysis that offers scenarios that will provide thoughtful data lenses to allow for evaluation of various scenarios, including a summary of estimated capital gains, turnover, and portfolio characteristics.

The SMA strategy is available in large and small company-equity asset classes, including both US and international. Generally, a minimum balance of $500,000 per asset-class strategy is required. The broad diversification we recommend is also possible at this asset level. This breakthrough methodology provides advisors with the ability to structure an investing approach that can be tailored to meet the specific goals, needs, and wants of their clients.

As we mentioned earlier, the advent of numerous technological breakthroughs has not only allowed for better evidence-based and faith-driven investing options, it has also made it more affordable.

> ### Looking for a Faith-Driven Advisor?
> One way to start is to go to kingdomadvisors.com. This website maintains a database of faith-driven advisors that have earned a Certified Kingdom Advisor (CKA®) professional designation. Their training is designed to provide financial planning and investment advice with a biblical worldview in mind. Simply search by geographic region in order to find an advisor near you.

SUMMARY: Faith-Driven Investing

In a survey conducted by the Christian Investment Forum, nearly 80 percent of Christian investors have expressed an interest in investing in Faith-Driven Investing. Sadly, nearly the same amount (77 percent) said that no advisor had ever mentioned Faith-Driven Investing to them. So, it seems clear that Christians are either (1) unaware, (2) don't know how, or (3) they are afraid of sacrificing return. Our purpose with this Postscript addition is to bring a greater awareness of this option.

Key Points

- **Faith-driven investing involves a conviction that God owns it all.** As Christ followers, that means we want to remove capital from the Enemy's campaign to redeploy for Kingdom purposes.
- **Faith-driven investing strategies are first rooted in an Evidence-Based Investing foundation.** The practical application is then designed to align an investor's personal values with their finances.

POSTSCRIPT: FAITH-DRIVEN INVESTING

- **By our estimates, there are nearly three thousand faith-driven advisors in the United States.** These "coaches" are equipped and ready to help with the implementation of biblical principles in your portfolio.

As stewards of what God has entrusted to us, we consider money to be a tool, a test, and a testimony. We believe there is no divide between the secular and the sacred. What we do in every aspect of our lives reflects not only who we are, but also *whose* we are. Therefore, an integration of faith and finance reflects our commitment to our Master.

In Chapter 9 where we introduced *Return on Legacy*®, over three thousand years ago, the writer of the book of Ecclesiastes wrote, "A good man leaves an inheritance to his children's children . . ."[7] It's widely considered that the "inheritance" spoken of here was more than just money. It held a broader definition in its original language dealing with wisdom, which is far more valuable.

If Faith-Driven Investing is important enough for you to pursue, then also consider the dividends it will pay to your family as they see what you truly value in life. In this, you can leave not only a greater inheritance of wisdom, but also an example of biblical stewardship lived out.

Using your investments as a statement of your faith is what true wealth management is all about. May it help you lead others to the Way of Eternal Life—the only thing that truly counts in the end.

Figure A.6

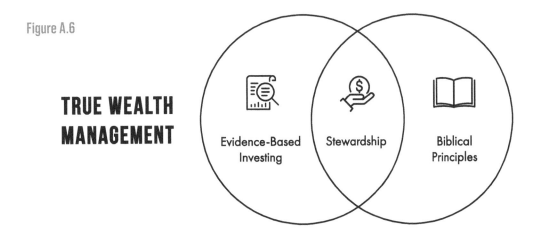

Acknowledgments

There are no books written by one person. It takes a team.

First things first, we want to thank our research associates, Dalton Smith and Logan Mulloy, for their countless hours of pouring over data and making all the little changes that make a difference. You're both clearly *wise beyond your years*.

A debt of gratitude is due to all the manuscript readers that improved this book immeasurably with their thoughtful suggestions.

In particular: Scott Socolofsky, Marilyn Adkinson, Kevin and Kim Walton, Reid Cuming, Erik Wagner, Joel Holyoak, Bill Braden, Vicki Weir, Frank and Pat Gilstrap, Micky Reeves, Nizie Whiddon, Jaime and Melissa Grunlan, Debra Fowler, Johnathan Whiddon, David and Diane Breeding, and Danny England. The investment of your valuable time in our efforts was not only greatly appreciated but also both flattering and humbling.

We also extend our sincere appreciation to Brown Books Publishing Group. Nobody does it like Milli Brown, Tom Reale, and their exceptional band of true professionals. Our project manager, Brittany Griffiths, along with Olivia Haase, Danny Whitworth, Ashley Mix, and Kimberly Gentry provided just the right touches to make this book better than we ever believed possible.

We especially want to thank our "most importants." Our lovely wives, Nizie Whiddon and Kimberly Gentry, who allowed us some extended hours during this year-long project. And also our dozen kids (between us—including in-laws), who are our pride and joy.

Finally, we want to thank our Lord . . . "in whom we live, and breathe, and have our very being."

James N. Whiddon and Matthew L. Gentry

Glossary

active management: The system of investment management that is dependent on predicting market and security movements (timing) and selection (picking).

asset classes: A grouping of investments that exhibit similar characteristics and are subject to the same laws and regulations.

bear market: Sustained periods of downward trending stock prices as measured by a 20 percent decline from near-term highs.

bull market: An environment in securities markets characterized by rising prices for a sustained period of time.

charting: A method to visualize the price action by plotting the historical market data of the underlying financial instrument on a graph.

data mining: The extraction of hidden predictive information from large databases.

direct pay: Money paid exclusively from a client directly to an advisory firm for financial advice. Direct pay is different from the entrenched Wall Street system of indirect payments, subsidies, and sales commissions.

efficient analyst paradox: Logical conclusion that the work of many highly skilled securities analysts will ensure efficient market prices, thus making those same skilled analysts unable to consistently find undervalued stocks.

evidence: That which makes plain or clear; ground for belief; proof.

Evidence-Based Investing: An investing approach that analyzes factual and time-tested historical data and applies it in a systematic manner rather than trying to speculate or outguess other market participants.

fiduciary: Advisors acting in the best interests of their client and disclosing any real or implied conflicts of interest. This is generally a higher standard than is customary in the financial services industry.

Fundamental Stock Analysis: Attempts to identify stocks offering strong growth potential at a good price by examining the underlying company's business as well as conditions within its industry or in the broader economy.

inalienable wealth: The concept which allows that the prosperity which is freely available via capital markets is incapable of being alienated, surrendered, transferred, or otherwise forfeited without the consent of a free market participant. An investor gives up the right to inalienable wealth when they succumb to the tyrannical Wall Street financial complex and its failed methodologies.

independent advisor: An advisor who is not employed or related in any way to brokerage houses, banks, or other financial institutions that may profit from offering incentives to advisors for recommending particular products. An independent advisor will be associated with a fee-based Registered Investment Advisor (RIA).

inflation: A general increase in prices and fall in the purchasing value of money.

institutional asset-class funds: Low-cost no-load mutual funds designed to represent whole asset classes as defined by Modern Portfolio Theory. Characteristically, they maintain their asset class integrity so that diversification remains consistent. These funds are often used by large institutional investors (such as pension and scholarship funds) and by the clients of many independent advisors.

large cap (company size): A company with a market capitalization value of more than $10 billion.

loss-plus-tax trap: The dilemma created when an investor seeks to avoid current long-term capital gains taxes on low basis investments instead of paying the taxes currently and implementing the consistent portfolio approach known as an Evidence-Based portfolio. This hesitation can lead to a loss of value in the securities he/she is holding as well as an eventual tax on the remaining gain when the security is sold, thus creating a double-loss situation.

market correction: A market decline that is more than 10 percent, but less than 20 percent.

market return: Nothing more, nothing less than the return readily available when investors efficiently harness the power of capital markets.

misaligned interests: The financial interests of institutions and representatives who provide advice and investment products that are in direct or indirect conflict with the financial interests of the investor.

Modern Portfolio Theory (MPT): Research in finance over the last seventy-plus years that relates to the risk and return characteristics of various asset classes when they are combined to create investment

mutual fund: A financial vehicle that pools assets from shareholders to invest in securities like stocks, bonds, real estate, money market instruments, and other assets.

periodic rebalancing: Adjusting the weightings of the different asset classes in your investment portfolio.

portfolio: A collection of financial investments like stocks, bonds, commodities, cash, and cash equivalents, including closed-end funds and exchange-traded funds (ETFs).

portfolio benchmark: Often a market index, a benchmark allows investors to gauge the relative performance of their portfolios in regards to both risk and return.

proprietary product: Products designed, manufactured, and managed by institutions whose representatives then recommend them to investors. Proprietary products often have higher costs and can have penalties for selling, which keep investors tied to the products.

regression to the mean: A statistical concept that refers to the fact that if one sample of a random variable is extreme, the next sampling of the same random variable is likely to be closer to its mean.

recession: A significant, widespread, and prolonged downturn in economic activity; is usually classified as two consecutive quarters of decline in gross domestic product (GDP).

security: Investment instruments such as stocks, bonds, or other tradable derivatives in open free markets.

small cap (company size): A stock from a public company whose total market value, or market capitalization, is about $300 million to $2 billion.

superdiversification: The high degree of portfolio diversification that occurs when broad and deep representation of the capital markets in the form of individual securities number in the thousands.

tax-loss harvesting: The timely selling of securities at a loss to offset the amount of capital gains tax due on the sale of other securities at a profit.

wealth: The value of one's time, talents, treasures, and relationships; abundance.

Notes

Introduction

1. "Top 10 Life Lessons From Warren Buffett." Forbes. Forbes Magazine, October 4, 2015. https://www.forbes.com/pictures/eede45imgh/there-seems-to-be-some-p/?sh=3651995c3f86.

Chapter 1

1. Christi Edwards. "News, Bond Markets Are Different." Bizjournals.com, February 10, 2012. https://www.bizjournals.com/nashville/print-edition/2012/02/10/news-bond-markets-are-different.html.
2. "Dow Jones Industrial Average Price, Real-Time Quote & News." Google Finance. Google. Accessed January 30, 202 3. https://www.google.com/finance/quote/.DJI:INDEXDJX?sa=X&ved=2ahUKEwiqhfSWhuH8AhWtnGoFHaHODHcQ3ecFegQILhAg&window=5Y.
3. Kimberly Amadeo. "How Did the 2020 Stock Market Crash Compare with Others?" The Balance, May 4, 2022. https://www.thebalance.com/fundamentals-of-the-2020-market-crash-4799950.
4. "The Rewarding Distribution of US Stock Market Returns." My.dimensional.com. May 2022. https://my.dimensional.com/dfsmedia/f27f1cc5b9674653938eb84ff8006d8c/92533-source/the-rewarding-distribution-of-us-stock-market-returns.pdf.
5. "Recession, or No Recession? the Latest Economic Data, in Context." chartr.co, July 29, 2022. https://www.chartr.co/stories/2022-07-29-1-us-economy-second-quarter-of-negative-growth.
6. Elyse Ausenbaugh. "The Case for (Always) Staying Invested." Credit Card, Mortgage, Banking, Auto, February 18, 2022. https://www.chase.com/personal/investments/learning-and-insights/article/tmt-february-eighteen-twenty-two.

7. "Bulls, Bears, and Long-Term Benefits of Stock Investing." My.dimensional.com. April 2022. https://my.dimensional.com/dfsmedia/f27f1cc5b9674653938eb84ff8006d8c/39602-source/bulls-bears-and-long-term-benefits-of-stock-investing.pdf.
8. Shah Gilani. "The Four Most Dangerous Words in Investing." MarketWatch. MarketWatch, March 1, 2011. https://www.marketwatch.com/story/four-most-dangerous-words-in-investing-2011-03-01.
9. Dimensional Fund Advisors. "Matrix Book 2022," Pg. 17, April 2022. https://static1.squarespace.com/static/5a29de13e5dd5b5fb7021e6c/t/62870fac4a7f90402dc03313/1653018551921/us_matrix-book-2022.pdf.
10. Sean Williams. "How Long Do Stock Market Corrections Last?" The Motley Fool. The Motley Fool, March 20, 2022. https://www.fool.com/investing/2022/03/20/how-long-do-stock-market-corrections-last/.
11. Photo courtesy of NASA Goddard Space Flight Center from Greenbelt, MD, USA.
12. "Korea, North—The World Factbook." Central Intelligence Agency. Central Intelligence Agency, January 11, 2023. https://www.cia.gov/the-world-factbook/countries/korea-north/.

Chapter 2

1. Mark Twain. *The Tragedy of Pudd'nhead Wilson*. American Publishing Company, 1894
2. Victor Fleming, director. *The Wizard of* Oz. Metro-Goldwyn-Mayer. 1939. 1 hr., 42 min. https://www.warnerbros.com/movies/wizard-oz.
3. "The Dangers of Portfolio Tinkering." Private Wealth Management. RW Baird Wealth, October 27, 2020. https://www.bairdwealth.com/insights/wealth-management-perspectives/2020/10/the-dangers-of-portfolio-tinkering/.
4. "Timing the Market Is Impossible." Hartford Funds, October 3, 2022. https://www.hartfordfunds.com/practice-management/client-conversations/managing-volatility/timing-the-market-is-impossible.html.
5. Ibid
6. Michael Lear-Olimpi, ed. "Spatial Disorientation Cause of Kennedy Plane Crash." Logistics Online. Accessed January 30, 2023. https://www.logisticsonline.com/doc/spatial-disorientation-cause-of-kennedy-plane-0001.
7. "Sketch Overview: Is Now a Good Time to Invest." My.dimensional.com. April 2022. https://my.dimensional.com/dfsmedia/f27f1cc5b9674653938eb84ff8006d8c/25546-source/sketch-overview-is-now-a-good-time-to-invest.pdf.
8. Ibid
9. Voltaire. *Dictionnaire philosophique portatif*. 1764

Chapter 3

1. "A Quote by Sean Kernan." Goodreads. Goodreads. Accessed January 31, 2023. https://www.goodreads.com/quotes/10672929-they-say-the-lottery-is-a-tax-on-people-who.
2. Burton G. Malkiel. *A Random Walk Down Wall Street: The Time-Tested Strategy for Successful Investing*. Twelfth ed. New York: W. W. Norton & Company, 2020.
3. Frederick E. Allen. "Cat Beats Professionals at Stock Picking." Forbes. Forbes Magazine, January 16, 2013. https://www.forbes.com/sites/frederickallen/2013/01/15/cat-beats-professionals-at-stock-picking/?sh=5cdf467a621a.
4. "What Are Mutual Funds?" Fidelity. Accessed January 30, 2023. https://www.fidelity.com/learning-center/investment-products/mutual-funds/what-are-mutual-funds.
5. Gabe Alpert. "The 5 Best-Performing Stocks of the Past 20 Years." Investopedia. Investopedia, July 13, 2022. https://www.investopedia.com/articles/investing/022716/5-best-performing-stocks-last-20-years-gmcr-celg.asp.
6. Ibid
7. James N. Whiddon. *Wealth without Worry: The Methods of Wall Street Exposed*. Dallas, TX: Brown Books Publishing Group, 2005. (Figure 3.2)
8. My.Dimensional.com. "Randomness of Returns." PowerPoint Presentation, 2022.
9. "2022 Index of Economic Freedom." Index of Economic Freedom: Promoting Economic Opportunity and Prosperity by Country. Accessed January 30, 2023. https://www.heritage.org/index/.
10. My.Dimensional.com. "Randomness of Returns." PowerPoint Presentation, 2022.
11. Ibid
12. Tim Edwards, Anu R. Ganti, Joe Nelesen, and David Di Gioia. "U.S. Persistence Scorecard Mid-Year 2022 ." S&P Global. Accessed January 30, 2023. https://www.spglobal.com/spdji/en/documents/spiva/persistence-scorecard-mid-year-2022.pdf.
13. Ibid
14. Ibid

Chapter 4

1. Shahid Mahmood. "The Motion of Heavenly Bodies." HuffPost. HuffPost, November 5, 2012. https://www.huffpost.com/entry/the-motion-of-heavenly-bo_b_1853969.
2. Charles Mackay. *Extraordinary Popular Delusions and the Madness of Crowds*. Reprint Edition. CreateSpace Independent Publishing Platform, 2011.
3. "Dutch Tulip Bulb Market Bubble." Corporate Finance Institute, January 9, 2023. https://corporatefinanceinstitute.com/resources/economics/dutch-tulip-bulb-market-bubble/.

4. Alex Steger. "The Rec List: How Many Managers Invest in Their Own Funds?" Pro Buyer. Citywire, October 26, 2020. https://citywire.com/pro-buyer/news/the-rec-list-how-many-managers-invest-in-their-own-funds/a1414253.
5. "Number of U.S. Mutual Funds 1997-2021." Statista, June 28, 2022. https://www.statista.com/statistics/255590/number-of-mutual-fund-companies-in-the-united-states/.
6. James N. Whiddon. *Wealth without Worry: The Methods of Wall Street Exposed.* Dallas, TX: Brown Books Publishing Group, 2005.
7. Ibid
8. Ibid
9. Rick Suter. "USA Today Ad Meter Returns for 35th Installment of Rating Super Bowl Commercials. What to Know." USA Today. Gannett Satellite Information Network, January 23, 2023. https://www.usatoday.com/story/sports/Ad-Meter/2023/01/23/rating-super-bowl-commercials-usa-today-ad-meter-returns/51216133/.
10. Henry Blodget. "Streetwise: A scandal waiting to happen," *Euromoney Magazine*, December 2004.

Chapter 5

1. Eccles. 11:2, (New American Standard).
2. Dimensional Fund Advisors. "Matrix Book 2022," April 2022. https://static1.squarespace.com/static/5a29de13e5dd5b5fb7021e6c/t/62870fac4a7f90402dc03313/1653018551921/us_matrix-book-2022.pdf.
3. David Hunkar. "U.S. Equity vs. International Equity 5-Year Rolling Returns: Chart." Topforeignstocks.com, January 24, 2022. https://topforeignstocks.com/2022/01/24/u-s-equity-vs-international-equity-5-year-rolling-returns-chart/.
4. Mt 7:25 (English Standard Version)
5. Harry Markowitz. "Portfolio Selection," *The Journal of Finance*, pp. 77-91. March 1952
6. "Jared Morton Designs." JARED MORTON DESIGNS. http://www.jaredmorton.com/.
7. E. Napoletano. "Expense Ratio: The Fee You Pay for Funds." Edited by Benjamin Curry. Forbes. Forbes Magazine, December 6, 2022. https://www.forbes.com/advisor/investing/what-is-expense-ratio/.
8. Stephan A. Abraham. "Turnover Ratios and Fund Quality." Investopedia. Investopedia, August 1, 2022. https://www.investopedia.com/articles/mutualfund/09/mutual-fund-turnover-rate.asp#:~:text=Turnover%20and%20Mutual%20Fund%20Quality,-Mutual%20fund%20turnover&text=You%20may%20discover%20that%20your,28%2C%202019.
9. "King Solomon." King Solomon. https://www.jewishvirtuallibrary.org/king-solomon.

NOTES

Chapter 6

1. John Dalberg-Acton Quotes. BrainyQuote.com, BrainyMedia Inc, 2023. https://www.brainyquote.com/quotes/john_dalbergacton_154525, accessed January 30, 2023.
2. Dimensional Fund Advisors. "Matrix Book 2022," April 2022. https://static1.squarespace.com/static/5a29de13e5dd5b5fb7021e6c/t/62870fac4a7f90402dc03313/1653018551921/us_matrix-book-2022.pdf.
3. Ibid
4. Ibid
5. Ibid
6. My.Dimensional.com. "Master Slide Deck." PowerPoint Presentation, Slide 130, 2022.
7. My.Dimensional.com. "Master Slide Deck." PowerPoint Presentation, Slide 131, 2022.
8. My.Dimensional.com. "Master Slide Deck." PowerPoint Presentation, Slide 132, 2022.
9. Robert Novy-Marx. "The Other Side of Value: The Gross Profitability Premium," June 2012. http://rnm.simon.rochester.edu/research/OSoV.pdf.
10. James N. Whiddon. *Wealth without Worry: The Methods of Wall Street Exposed.* Dallas, TX: Brown Books Publishing Group, 2005.
11. Dimensional Fund Advisors. "Matrix Book 2022," April 2022. https://static1.squarespace.com/static/5a29de13e5dd5b5fb7021e6c/t/62870fac4a7f90402dc03313/1653018551921/us_matrix-book-2022.pdf.

Chapter 7

1. Aristotle Quotes. BrainyQuote.com, BrainyMedia Inc, 2023. https://www.brainyquote.com/quotes/aristotle_117887, accessed January 30, 2023.
2. "Siren." Encyclopedia Britannica. Encyclopedia Britannica, inc., July 20, 1998. https://www.britannica.com/topic/Siren-Greek-mythology.
3. John Stuart Mill. "Speech on Perfectibility." Speech, Debating Society, 1828.
4. Brian J. Bloch. "Black Swan Events and Investment." Investopedia. Investopedia, September 29, 2022. https://www.investopedia.com/articles/trading/11/black-swan-events-investing.asp.
5. Ibid
6. "Epidemics and Stock Market Performance." First Trust Portfolios, February 24, 2020. https://static.fmgsuite.com/media/documents/349cbb9f-4db7-4078-bb6f-156f6d26ea97.pdf.
7. Joe Gromelski. "NFL Coaching Great Marv Levy Remembers the Euphoria of V-J Day." Stars and Stripes, September 2, 2017. https://www.stripes.com/veterans/nfl-coaching-great-marv-levy-remembers-the-euphoria-of-v-j-day-1.485820.

8. Dimensional Fund Advisors. "Matrix Book 2022," April 2022. https://static1.squarespace.com/static/5a29de13e5dd5b5fb7021e6c/t/62870fac4a7f90402dc03313/1653018551921/us_matrix-book-2022.pdf.
9. "How Much Impact Does the President Have on Stocks." My.dimensional.com. Accessed January 30, 2023. https://my.dimensional.com/how-much-impact-does-the-president-have-on-stocks.
10. Jay Martin. "Buffett Made 95% of His Wealth after the Age of 65." Cambridge House International, August 28, 2020. https://cambridgehouse.com/news/8730/warren-buffett-will-die-with-billions
11. Dimensional Fund Advisors. "Matrix Book 2022," April 2022. https://static1.squarespace.com/static/5a29de13e5dd5b5fb7021e6c/t/62870fac4a7f90402dc03313/1653018551921/us_matrix-book-2022.pdf.

Chapter 8

1. Leo Tolstoy. *War and Peace*. The Russian Messenger, 1869
2. Hendrik de Vries. "An Unexpected Solution to the High Failure Rate among New Advisors." VettaFi Advisor Perspectives, February 15, 2022. https://www.advisorperspectives.com/articles/2022/02/15/an-unexpected-solution-to-the-high-failure-rate-among-new-advisors.
3. Plato. *Protagoras*. 380 B.C.E.
4. Lewis Carroll. *Alice's Adventures in Wonderland*. The Claredon Press, 1865.
5. Michael Kitces. "Managing Sequence Risk: Bucket Strategies VS TOTAL RETURN." Nerd's Eye View | Kitces.com, February 1, 2019. https://www.kitces.com/blog/managing-sequence-of-return-risk-with-bucket-strategies-vs-a-total-return-rebalancing-approach/.

Chapter 9

1. Jay Kristoff. *Darkdawn: Book Three of the Nevernight Chronicle*. St. Martin's Press, 2019.
2. Larry Ballard. "MULTIGENERATIONAL LEGACIES—THE STORY OF JONATHAN EDWARDS." YWAM Family Ministries Intl, July 1, 2017. https://www.ywam-fmi.org/news/multigenerational-legacies-the-story-of-jonathan-edwards/.
3. Jeffrey Mason. *Dad, I Want to Hear Your Story: A Father's Guided Journal to Share His Life & His Love*. EYP Publishing. 2019.
4. Questions About Me. *Tell Me Your Life Story, Grandpa*. Questions About Me, 2021.

Afterword

5. "Times Call for Liberal Action, Says Kennedy." *Lodi News-Sentinel*, May 13, 1961. https://news.google.com/newspapers?id=QOgzAAAAIBAJ&sjid=g4HAAAAIBAJ&dq=americans+for+democratic+action&pg=7056%2C2944411.

Postscript

1. Prov 3:9 (ESV)
2. Psm 19:1 (New King James Version)
3. Mt 25:14–30 (ESV)
4. Rachel McDonough. "The Stewardship of Faith-Based Investing." Essay. In Investing and Faith: The Impact of Faith-Based Investing, edited by Steve French, 77–88. Independently Published, 2019.
5. Psm 97:10 (ESV)
6. "When Screening Investments for Christian Values, Does Sin Win? An Impressive and Reassuring Revelation." Accessed January 30, 2023. https://www.briinstitute.com/backtest.pdf.
7. Prov 13:22 (NKJV)

Illustration Credits

Chapter 1

1. Figure 1.2. *Source:* Data from Google Finance, Dow Jones Industrial Average https://www.google.com/finance/quote/sa=X&ved=2ahUKEwiqhfSWhuH8AhWtnGoFHaHODHcQ3ecFegQILhAg&window=5Y
2. Figure 1.3. CRSP data provided by the Center for Research in Security Prices, University of Chicago https://my.dimensional.com/dfsmedia/f27f1cc5b9674653938eb84ff8006d8c/92533-source/the-rewarding-distribution-of-us-stock-market-returns.pdf
3. Figure 1.4. *Source:* Data from Bureau of Economic Analysis https://www.chartr.co/stories/2022-07-29-1-us-economy-second-quarter-of-negative-growth
4. Figure 1.5. *Source:* Data from J.P. Morgan Private Bank. FactSet. [1] Cumulative total returns for S&P 500 are calculated from December 31 of the year prior to January 31, 2022. https://www.chase.com/personal/investments/learning-and-insights/article/tmt-february-eighteen-twenty-two
5. Figure 1.6. *Source:* Data from S&P data © 2022 S&P Dow Jones Indices LLC, a division of S&P Global. https://my.dimensional.com/dfsmedia/f27f1cc5b9674653938eb84ff8006d8c/39602-source/bulls-bears-and-long-term-benefits-of-stock-investing.pdf
6. Figure 1.7. *Source:* Data from Dimensional Fund Advisors, Matrix Book 2022, Pg. 17
7. Figure 1.9. *Sources:* Data from Yardeni Research; Table from The Motley Fool https://www.fool.com/investing/2022/03/20/how-long-do-stock-market-corrections-last/
8. Figure 1.10. Photo of North and South Korea. Image is in the public domain, courtesy of NASA

Chapter 2

1. Figure 2.4. *Sources*: Data from Ned Davis Research, Morningstar, and Hartford Funds, 2/22. https://www.hartfordfunds.com/practice-management/client-conversations/managing-volatility/timing-the-market-is-impossible.html

2. Figure 2.5. Ibid
3. Figure 2.6. *Source:* Data from S&P 500 Total Returns Index. S&P data© 2022 S&P Dow Jones Indices LLC, a division of S&P Global; S&P Total Return Index, Stocks, Bonds, Bills and Inflation Yearbook™, Ibbotson Associates, Chicago. https://my.dimensional.com/dfsmedia/f27f1cc5b9674653938eb84ff8006d8c/25546-source/sketch-overview-is-now-a-good-time-to-invest.pdf
4. Figure 2.7. Ibid

Chapter 3

1. Figure 3.2. *Source:* Data from Dimensional Fund Advisor
2. Figure 3.3. *Source:* Data from MSCI data© MSCI, 2022 https://my.dimensional.com/dfsmedia/f27f1cc5b9674653938eb84ff8006d8c/592-source/randomness-of-returns.pptx
3. Figure 3.4. *Source:* Data from MSCI and S&P Dow Jones Indices LLC, a division of S&P Global. MSCI data© MSCI 2022 https://my.dimensional.com/dfsmedia/f27f1cc5b9674653938eb84ff8006d8c/592-source/randomness-of-returns.pptx
4. Figure 3.5. Ibid
5. Figure 3.6. *Source:* Data from S&P Dow Jones Indices LLC, CRSP https://www.spglobal.com/spdji/en/documents/spiva/persistence-scorecard-mid-year-2022.pdf
6. Figure 3.7. Ibid
7. Figure 3.8. Ibid

Chapter 4

1. Figure 4.1. *Source:* Data from Morningstar Principia Pro Database as of December 31, 2004.
2. Figure 4.2. Ibid
3. Figure 4.3. Ibid
4. Figure 4.4. *Source:* Data from Bogle Financial Markets Research Center

Chapter 5

1. Figure 5.4. *Source:* Data from Dimensional Fund Advisors Matrix Book 2022, Pg. 74-75.
2. Figure 5.5. *Sources*: Data from Morningstar and Hartford Funds, 10/21. (needs to be recreated) https://topforeignstocks.com/2022/01/24/u-s-equity-vs-international-equity-5-year-rolling-returns-chart/

Chapter 6

1. Figure 6.2. *Source:* Data from Dimensional Fund Advisors Matrix Book 2022
2. Figure 6.3. Ibid

ILLUSTRATION CREDITS

3. Figure 6.4. Ibid
4. Figure 6.5. Ibid
5. Figure 6.6. CC by Reichsbanksdirektorium
6. Figure 6.7. *Source:* Data from S&P data © 2022 S&P Dow Jones Indices LLC, a division of S&P Global
7. Figure 6.8. *Source:* Data from Fama/French US Value Research Index minus the Fama/French US Growth Research Index
8. Figure 6.9. *Source:* Data from Fama/French US High Profitability Index minus the Fama/French US Low Profitability Index
9. Figure 6.12. *Source:* Data from Dimensional Fund Advisor
10. Figure 6.13. *Source:* Data from Dimensional Core Wealth Index Models. Dimensional Fund Advisors Matrix Book 2022. Assumes tax-deferred retirement account.

Chapter 7

1. Figure 7.3. *Source:* Data from Bloomberg, as of 2/24/20. Month end numbers were used for the 6- and 12-month % change. http://static.fmgsuite.com/media/documents/349cbb9f-4db7-4078-bb6f-156f6d26ea97.pdf
2. Figure 7.4. *Source:* Data from Dimensional Fund Advisors Matrix Book 2022
3. Figure 7.5. *Source:* Data from S&P data © 2022 S&P Dow Jones Indices LLC, a division of S&P Global
4. Figure 7.8. *Source:* Data from Dimensional Fund Advisors. "Matrix Book 2022," April 2022. https://static1.squarespace.com/static/5a29de13e5dd5b5fb7021e6c/t/62870fac4a7f90402dc03313/1653018551921/us_matrix-book-2022.pdf.

Chapter 8

1. Figure 8.3. *Source:* Data from Michael Kitces. "Managing Sequence Risk: Bucket Strategies VS TOTAL RETURN." Nerd's Eye View | Kitces.com, February 1, 2019. https://www.kitces.com/blog/managing-sequence-of-return-risk-with-bucket-strategies-vs-a-total-return-rebalancing-approach/.

Postscript

1. Figure A.5. *Source:* Data from BRII, Bloomberg. The screened results presented in this document are simulated and do not correspond to any real investment product. Simulated performance data is hypothetical and provided for informational purposes only. It does not reflect actual performance and is gross of any fees. (Figure is exact data match) https://briinstitute.com/backtest.pdf.

About the Authors

James N. Whiddon

Jim is a Certified Financial Planner® practitioner and holds a Masters of Science degree in Financial Services from the American College in Philadelphia. Whiddon founded JWA Financial Group, Inc. in Dallas, Texas, and served as CEO for twenty-seven years before his firm was acquired in a merger in 2013. He subsequently cofounded and is CEO of Evidence Wealth LLC, an independent Registered Investment Advisory firm in Bryan, Texas. Whiddon is the author of six books, and his work has been quoted or seen in more than 350 publications and national media outlets, including *Fortune* magazine, the *Wall Street Journal*, and *CNBC*. He has also been a *FOX News Radio* contributor.

Originally from Amarillo, Texas, Jim was a member of the Corps of Cadets at Texas A&M University where he earned his undergraduate degree and served as a graduate assistant coach for the Aggie basketball team. He is a two-time recipient of the "Aggie 100 Award" from the Mays Center for Entrepreneurship. Whiddon also founded the Old School, which instructs students on "The 12 Keys to Professional Success," which he teaches in the Financial Planning Program at Texas A&M.

Matthew L. Gentry

After several years of working in the financial industry, Gentry founded Parity Financial Group LLC in 2015. He currently serves as President and COO of Evidence Wealth LLC in Bryan, Texas. Matt is a Certified Financial Planner® practitioner as well as a Certified Kingdom Advisor®.

Born and raised in Houston, Texas, Matt graduated from Texas A&M University in 2006 with a Bachelor's of Business Administration in Finance. He also earned a degree from Shepherds Theological Seminary in 2017. Matt's stated professional goal of "keeping his clients' success as the focal point of everything he does" has been his guiding principle.

Other Books by the Author

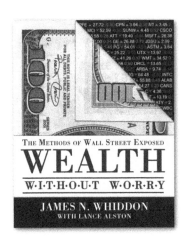
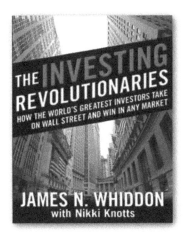

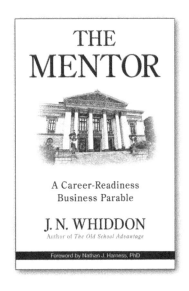